FROM NORTH LONDON

Edited by Lucy Jenkins

First published in Great Britain in 2000 by
YOUNG WRITERS
Remus House,
Coltsfoot Drive,
Woodston,
Peterborough, PE2 9JX
Telephone (01733) 890066

All Rights Reserved

Copyright Contributors 2000

HB ISBN 0 75431 864 8
SB ISBN 0 75431 865 6

FOREWORD

This year, the Young Writers' Future Voices competition proudly presents a showcase of the best poetic talent from over 42,000 up-and-coming writers nationwide.

Successful in continuing our aim of promoting writing and creativity in children, our regional anthologies give a vivid insight into the thoughts, emotions and experiences of today's younger generation, displaying their inventive writing in its originality.

The thought, effort, imagination and hard work put into each poem impressed us all and again the task of editing proved challenging due to the quality of entries received, but was nevertheless enjoyable. We hope you are as pleased as we are with the final selection and that you continue to enjoy *Future Voices From North London* for many years to come.

CONTENTS

Daphne Dionne Shanay Addo	1
Shrina Parmar	1
Emma Tuttlebury	2
Kayleigh Smithers	2

City & Islington College

Ruby Begum	3

Edmonton County School

Nikash Ramsorrun	4
Suzanne Coleman	5
Muesser Mehmet	5
Hollie Jones	6
Samuel Dean	6
Michael Lee Norwood	7
Christina Kashoumeri	7
Glenn Jenkins	8
Mark Longmuir	8
Katrina Constantinou	9
Sinem Saffet	9
Lucy Cogan	10
Sinem Halil	10
Ben Dingwall	11
Sarah Parsons	12
Megan Hallsworth	12
Anupa Thaker	13
Louisa Paschali	13
Bahar Huseyin	14

Hampstead School

Naomi Stoll	15
Rhian Davies	16
Arun Sethi	18
Keara Stewart	19
Abigail Hay	20

Haverstock School
- Ollie Haydon-Mulligan — 21

Kingsbury High School
- Hamed Shojanoori — 22
- Harry Wu — 23
- Himal Hirani — 23
- Dipal Patel — 24
- Rikesh Jani — 25
- Kavita Joshi — 26
- Vishaal Sachania — 27
- Anita Advani — 27
- Vikash Vekaria — 28
- Jaydene Sacha Harper — 28
- Para Manko — 29
- Stephanie Johnson — 30
- Urmila Kerai — 30
- Poonam Mepani — 31
- Krishma Vaghela — 32
- Mohsin Hussain — 33

St Mary's CE High School, Downage
- Dumisani Chirwa — 34
- Zeodora Dujmovic — 34
- Rachel Carmichael — 35
- Lavina Suthenthiran — 36
- Loretta King — 36
- Balaal Malik — 37
- Puneh Mohammed — 38
- Shamaine Boyce — 38
- George Johnston — 39
- Anthony Karanu Kabuba — 39
- Janine Wright — 40
- David Bell-Gam — 41
- Sarah J Shore — 42
- Jason Hardman — 43
- Shaz Forozan — 43
- Mathararaj Nithianantharajah — 44

Patrick Hickey	44
Harsha Patel	45
Olaolu Oloyede	46
Sam Layton	46
Katie Stimson	47
Jade Cottrell	48
Simon Sullivan	48
Christina McNamara	49
Payal Jolapara	50
Victor Matovu	50
Nilam Patel	51
Pasindu Silva	51
James Alexander Pettican	52
Ruth Matsunaga	52
Forum Shah	53
Dionne Benjamin	53
Faye Blair	54
Soléne Bhagwanani	55
Ricardo Reittie	55
Antonio Corbin	56
Jessica Ward	57
Prachi Mesvani	58
Samantha Burcher	59
Sabina McCulloch	60
Yasmin Putz	60
Catharine Bishop	61
Christopher Fennelly	61
Sandhya Ahuja	62
Gabrielle Brewster	62
Esha Massand	63
Michael Campbell	64
Onike Kanda	64
Rubee Variava	65
Carianne Wylie	65
Dilan Kanli	66
Waqar Kasker	66
Angie Wong	67
Andreas Charalambous	68

Tunde Hazzan	68
Vidusha Vijayakumar	69
Caroline Lowes	69
Dominic Beeput	70
Safeena Kadiri	70
Vikas Kapoor	71
Umar Ahmed	71
Carley Coles	72
Kelvin Gichohi	72
Lianne Cooper-Brown	73
James Mackie	73
Paul Langley	74
Charlene Wright	74
Christopher Barker	75
Leonella Dujmovic	75
Minal Wadhia	76
Louina Ajuo	77
Jerome Jefferson	78
Horacio Alberto Ortega Di Gregorio	78
Dana Al-Omari	79
Chelsea Hickey	80
Sarah Griffiths	80
Josephine Balfour	81
Reshma Patel	81
Natassa Charalambous	82
Loretta Henry	83
Zara Park	84
Sharmaine Mehar Malik	85
Darryn Davies	85
Christina Tseriotis	86
Tapiwa Agere	86
Alaba Badewa	87
Nicole Bandoo	87
Amy Chandler	88
Kimberley Briggs	88
Nivine Saleh	89
Natallie Lucien	89
Steph Phillips	90

Daniel Smith	91
Arjun Kumar Mittra	92
Tyrone Hemmings	93
Sim-Chung Tang	94
Motunrayo Onanuga	94
Flossie Tecson	95
Holly Dooley	96
Geu MacBullen	96
Daniel Plaistow	97
Imogen Katz	98
Marvin Davidson	98
Clare Lenton	99
Laura Payne	100
Bianca Fough	102
Chris Skordis	102
Rubina Pausker	103
Jason Fester	103
Michael Fowler	104
Subathra Sivanandan	104
Carla Powell	105
Jade Georgiou	106
Hannah Compton	107
Rochelle Davids	108
Jasmine Ahmed	108
Valery Katerinchuk	109
Raphael V Griffith	110
Velma Candy	110
Kunal Jadeja	111
Christine Neumann	112
Kamran Golami	112
Kieren Russell	113
Michael Mazur	114
Philip Brian Powis-Vasey	114
Louis Mateega	115
Oki Sampurno	116
Amma Ansomaa Brefo	116
Rajiv Varsani	117
Valerie Usuanlele-Beckley	118

James Osborn	118
Gemma Williams	119
Nicola Stephenson	119
Scott Shelley	120
Mark Davie	120
Leon Gordon-Ailey	121
Priya Makwana	122
Jeremy Boamah	122

South Hampstead High School

Annabel Grossman	123
Selina Tang	124
Venetia Rainey	125
Natalie Simpson-Hassell	126
Rebecca Perlman	127
Saba Yussouf	128
Elizabeth Elster	129
Rebecca Herman	130
Stephanie Horn	131
Lauren Cooney	132
Elizabeth Rawlings	133
Danielle Gertner	134
Alice Edgerley	135
Isobel Freeman	136
Laura Vignoles	137
Tatiana Los	138
Sabrina Paramesh	138
Leora Graham	139
Stefanie Stavri	140
Kate Evangeli	141
Lina Harfouche	142
Yasemin Dil	142
Julia Gibson	143
Georgina Cox	144
Jessica Oughton	144
Katherine Phoenix	145
Natasha Kahn	146
Hannah Gross	147

Noor Nanji	148
Siobhan Toone	148
Emma Hindley	149
Louise Simpson	150
Susannah Buckler	150
Milica Filimonovic	151
Eva Tausig	152
Ruthie Samuel	154
Rebecca Moodey	154
Laura Elvin	155
Rachel Stratton	156
Sarah Bolsom-Morris	157
Jessie Lieberson	158
Sara Nielsen-Dzumhur	159
Jessica Howard	160
Elizabeth Metliss	161
Georgina Ely	162
Ishita Menta	163
Emily Zitcer	164
Rachel Lob-Levyt	165

White Hart Lane School

Harun Abdi Hassan	165
Kazan Tawfiq	166
Jamila Cunningham	166
Rasika Amarasinghe	167
Jennifer Kan	168
Sibel Sonara	168
Laamaray Rhoden	169
Siohvan Cleo Crombie	170
Shubhana Zubair Mohammed	170
Mary Sofolabo	171

The Poems

The Sea

As I sit beside the sea
I wonder how it could be
That there's no place on earth
As peaceful as the sea.

As I curl my toes in the golden sand
And stroke it with my hand
The birds sing a secret
Tune which sends my heart
Winging over and over again.

The sun is shining
Its radiant colours glow
It's not the ceiling
Yet it's not on the floor
More powerful than any king or queen.

It pains me to think
That this peace of heaven
May never be experienced again
Not by man, woman, boy, girl
Or even I.

Daphne Dionne Shanay Addo (11)

I Felt You

I felt you speaking in my dreams but not a sound was heard,
I felt you were close to me but not a soul was seen.
I spoke to you knowing that it will be heard.
I loved you thinking you loved me too.
I almost touched the sky with your hand in mine.
I felt all the peace and quiet when I was close to you.
I felt I had all the happiness when you looked at me once,
I went crazy when you said few words to me.

Shrina Parmar (15)

WHO ARE WE?

Some are thin, some are fat,
Some wear caps and some wear hats,
Some have beards and some do not,
Some have so much hair they get hot,
Some like cars, some like bikes,
Some like football and some like hikes,
Some are artists and like to paint
And some when decorating get in such a state,
Some drink tea and some drink beer,
When some come home they say 'Hello dear,'
Can you guess who they are?
Of course it is your papa.

Emma Tuttlebury (11)

HOMELESS

Cold and dark, as deep as the night,
Colours of dawn is my only light,
Torn and battered,
Weak and still,
People look down and ask if I'm ill.

Howling dogs lurk round the streets,
I huddle under my thin, grey sheet,
Small and scared,
Pale and white,
Hungry for love that would make my life right.

Kayleigh Smithers (10)

OBSESSION

There she stood with a sparkle in her eye
daunting to take her first step,
for that love had hit her heart.
Hit her hard that she felt it inside,
one look at him and she fell in love
with the man she will never have.
Tears to fill a river were shed for
it burned inside not seeing him eye to eye.
Day after day it becomes a losing battle
that one day she will have to give up.
She would dream about catching his every move
and following his every step
and stand on his pathway,
his pathway to life,
she would die for his love and give it all
but her love will not be returned.
He would be in her dreams,
he would be in her sleep and she
ever imagined he would be there to protect her.
She promised she will never let him go,
she said she loved him forever
that in her heart they will be together,
for she never believed her love had turned
to obsession.

Ruby Begum (17)
City & Islington College

OPHELIA

A life of twist and turns,
A life of love, hate, innocence and despair,
This is Ophelia's life in her very last breaths.
Reflected like a failed test paper
And a cause of death to her woeful father later
As she battles in vain to win Hamlet's heart.
Her heart shatters and falls apart
And when the news came from the door that Hamlet
Killed her father
Her love for beloved Hamlet drifted off like an elegant,
                                              snow white dove.
She runs to the stream fearing nothing but Hamlet .
She then picks off the delicate and fragile flowers off
The tree to represent her cruel life.
Rose for love
Daisies for childhood and innocence
And poppies for death
But no one recognised her purity and optimism.
With the water piercing her skin like a thousand daggers
She the damsel in no distress, but in despair waits for her
Life to come to a grinding halt and her body to decompose.
Then a flash of white brilliance came before her eyes
And recalled love, hate, innocence and deaths with her
Closing words and very last breath, she departures
From her existence.

Nikash Ramsorrun (13)
Edmonton County School

WATER DEATH

Silently crying, being loved in vain,
No family to talk to, no other love in my life.
Pain stabs my heart in grief and despair,
Depression strikes my life so I might as well go.

Walking to the river on this shallow afternoon
Picking up the daisies as I sit on the earth,
Leaning over the river to catch a lily,
I suddenly fall into the icy cold water.
What a great way to end my life
But where to next?
Will it be heaven?
Will it be hell?
Wherever I go, I'm going down, going down, going.

Suzanne Coleman (12)
Edmonton County School

THE STIMULATING CHOCOLATE!

The wrapper is smooth and slinky
You're lured to the appetising bar shape,
As you strip the chocolate off
Its green wrapper,
The creamy chocolate smells are
Released.
The temptation is almost painful.
As you put it near your mouth
The smell of the chocolate makes you
Feel sensational
The texture is so creamy, it's irresistible.
Then it's in your mouth! Mmm . . .

Muesser Mehmet (14)
Edmonton County School

JEWISH CAMPS

We are all ushered out the cattle train,
Many dead, most in pain,
3 days in darkness,
The light hurts our eyes,
We didn't know we were going to die,
We are in damp conditions, corpses everywhere,
Blood down the walls,
Blood on the floor,
We are stripped of our privacy,
Rights and strength,
Just living in filth and stench
It seems the end.
We are thin and bony,
Scrawny and skinny,
We are offered a shower,
Hurrah we say,
But little did we know,
It's our last day.

Hollie Jones (12)
Edmonton County School

LIFE AND DEATH

The cold dead waters surround the body of Ophelia,
Desolate air runs over the river onto her face,
Growing life all around her but still frozen death lying in the middle,
Her pale stone face sinks beneath the surface,
Exquisite silk of her dress spoiled by the icy waters,
The water covers her face, she takes her last breath,
Her heart beats its last beat but then stops, ending her unspoiled life,
All she showed was innocence but all she got was pain,
Loneliness of another life taken, but yet death has another victim.

Samuel Dean (13)
Edmonton County School

FALLING BOMBS

Banging on the door,
Banging, banging, banging!
Screaming, screaming,
Let me in, please, please, let me in!

Slowly the door swings open,
The bombs are falling,
Bang, bang,
The door slams shut,
With me outside.

I ran, I ran away,
But the bombs keep coming.
Shrapnel flying, flying through the air.
The shrapnel is flying,
It hits me!
And I am . . .

Michael Lee Norwood (12)
Edmonton County School

SOUL MATES

Sister, soul mate, closest friend,
The love shared between
Two sisters that will never end.
Sweetest smile, kindest face.
I never knew a girl with so much grace.
You saved my life but lost your own,
So much sorrow makes me fear
What have I done?
To the sweetest face
The little girl with so much grace.

Christina Kashoumeri (13)
Edmonton County School

OPHELIA

As she lay in the icy water
As she drifted away
There were no screams of any kind
No sigh of deadly pain.

As death came to grasp her life
To take it away from us
As she lay there in the flowing river
The heavens took her soul.

As the flowers watch over her
When she died without pain
Her white ghostly face
As it sinks beneath the air.

Blossoms around her water grave
Her silky white dress
Which runs over her pale skin
Now she is gone, she is no more.

Glenn Jenkins (12)
Edmonton County School

THE DEATH OF OPHELIA

In the gentle breezy wind, a faint tune travels.
As I walk to the river bank
I take one last look at the world I am going to leave behind,
As I lie in the freezing cold icy water.
I think of the people I loved
And the man that won't love me back
As I struggle to take my last breath I think of my father,
Who I will now be with once again.

Mark Longmuir (12)
Edmonton County School

OPHELIA

I'm lying in the water
Pretending I'm Ophelia
How much longer?
I'm starting to feel like her
I'm in that dress
That makes me feel old
All these flowers on my dress
They mean a lot to me
The poppy death
The pansies loving in vain
The daisies innocence
The roses love
Flowers surround me
In freezing water
What am I going to do next?

Katrina Constantinou (12)
Edmonton County School

DYING SLOWLY

A rose between us gets broken,
My father is gone, I feel so depressed.
My heart is broken so I slowly fall
Down the cold, iced river.

The river flows in calm gentle waves,
I just lie there so peaceful and still,
Can't bare to help myself.

My puffy dress takes me beyond by
Floating on the river.
The flowers round me keep me safe,
The poppy near me is the sign of death.

Sinem Saffet (12)
Edmonton County School

OPHELIA

I want him to love me,
Even if it was just a little.
I want him to care for me as I care for him,
There's no point living if I can't be with him.
He's breaking my heart why can't he see that?
I'll go down to the river to dream about him,
To smell the elegant flowers
And the soft breeze to flow around my body.
Sitting by the river, dreaming about him.
I feel a slight push and another.
I don't hold back,
Just thinking
'This will make him think of me.'
I fall into the river.
I think to myself as I take my last breath,
He will know how much I loved him,
By the flowers which lay around
My hurting body.

Lucy Cogan (12)
Edmonton County School

FRIENDS

If you're feeling down
Or even hurt inside
A friend should always be there
To make you feel alright.

If you've got some problems
Even if they're big ones.
A friend should always be there
To give you good advice.

Someone you can talk to
Someone who will care
Someone you can share problems with
Who will listen and always be there.

This is what a friend is
A friend that you can trust
A friend should always be there
A good friend is a must.

Sinem Halil (13)
Edmonton County School

WAR

Oh what a shameful world it is,
Waging wars, for no evident reason.
Then you hear the wails of men,
Being hanged for suspected treason.

Poor people enduring this war,
They try to get away.
'Bang, bang' you hear in the distance,
The people on the grass, dead they lie.

Buildings blown out with pipe bombs,
The ground scarred with blood.
Then you see a bomb in front,
'Phew, it's just a dud.'

Then you hear of peace out here,
The elation of people 'Hooray!'
The handshakes of people are truly a sight,
Just to start again another day.

Ben Dingwall (13)
Edmonton County School

SILENT DEATH

Heartbreak depression
It's time for me to go
Down to the bottom of the river,
All the way down below.

Being loved in vain
No one cares
Whether I'm dead or alive,
As I silently cry
So no one will hear,
I hope I go to heaven,
Even though I might of
Committed suicide.

Sarah Parsons (12)
Edmonton County School

PARTY TIME

Going around to a friends house,
Getting changed,
Eating chips and pizza,
Leaving the house in a brand new BMW,
Arriving at the disco,
Greeting your friends,
Dancing around and around,
Jumping to the beat,
Music's finished,
Party's over,
Walking home alone,
Silence,
Only memories left.

Megan Hallsworth (13)
Edmonton County School

HE'S THE ONE!

He looked at me in class today,
He looked at me deep,
I felt his eyes on me,
They were quite steep.

I looked at him back today,
I got all tingly,
His small, tight eyes,
Staring at me.

At first I was scared,
But now I know,
We were meant to be.

Anupa Thaker (13)
Edmonton County School

MY LOVE

I glanced in his direction,
Who was he standing there?
He looked in my direction,
We both began to stare.
I felt I knew the man inside him,
I felt a moment of pleasure.
This man that I thought I did not know,
Was a once in a lifetime treasure.
Now, no longer do I know him,
No longer do we stare.
No longer do I see him,
But my love for him is still there.

Louisa Paschali (14)
Edmonton County School

OR IS IT!

We're all part of a racist community,
But how can this be?
Is it because
We all have our colour and personality
Or is it according to our gender
Or maybe our ethnic culture
Or maybe it's just our unstable structure?
The one we were born with,
The one we all grew up with,
The one they made us!
They gave us our name and the strength
We ourselves should gain,
But at the end of the day,
We grew up in pain and life to us
May seem vain,
But have we ever thought,
It was us who brought - the fear?
Are we all the same?
Do we all scare the same?
Do we all think that life's full of
Pain and vain,
Or is it just us alone who have
Grown to be scared of ourselves and each other?
Or is it!

Bahar Huseyin (13)
Edmonton County School

Fire In Its Eyes

The tiger awakens from his slumber,
Heavy rain pounding his coat.
The twilight hits leaves thrashing in the wind.
Lazily he stretches, rises to his feet.
His yawn ensures a breath of the sweet spiced air
that hangs all around.
Lightning streaks through the trees,
Its stark light being shot at the forest.
Crackling!
His ears prick up,
With arched back he creeps towards the noise.
There a creature waits;
Its numerous arms snatching at the air,
Its bright light forces the tiger to drop his stare,
It hisses and cracks, spitting out sparks.
The tiger roars,
Clawing, swiping desperately,
Forced surrender never having been encountered.
Still the creature grows,
Engulfing the tiger's pride with its surroundings.
Defeat.
Seething with rage he turns,
Teeth bared.
A warning to watchers,
For to them he is still 'King of the Jungle.'

Naomi Stoll (14)
Hampstead School

T.E.E.N Spells Trouble

As soon as I come down the stairs,
She's there, looking me up and down.
'You're not going out dressed like that.'
My smile turns into a frown.

'It took ages to find this outfit,' I say,
'You'll never believe how long.
You used to dress like this in your day, mum,
Personally, I don't see what's wrong.'

'Of course you don't my dear,' she smiles,
She's taking the mick out of me.
'Girls these days are looking like tarts.
You'll get followed around, you'll see.'

'How do you know that's not what I want?
Maybe I like how I look.
I'm probably not the daughter you wanted,
Walking 'round, reading poetry books.'

She ignores my pleas and my whiny voice.
'Go and put on something new.
You can't pretend that belt's a skirt,
You don't want to catch a cold, do you?'

I look up at her and put on a face.
'You just don't understand.'
'Of course I do, sweetheart,' she says
'Clothes like that should be banned.'

'You look much nicer in trousers and shirts.
Go on, get upstairs.'
I glare at her as she pushes me out.
'God, you're so unfair.'

'Oh darling,' she calls as I run to my room,
'What?' I shout, in a mood.
'There's a sensible sweater in your drawer,
Get changed and come down for some food.'

'Then an idea hits me fast.
'Of course, how could I be so dumb?'
I pull on my jeans over my outfit,
And go down to speak with my mum.

'Mum,' I say, in my sweetest of voices
'I'm going out to see Kate.
Don't bother staying up for me,
I'll be coming home quite late.'

She nods absentmindedly in my direction
'Be home by two, if not before.'
I squeak, 'yes' trying to suppress my grin,
Then I walk confidently out of the door.

Rhian Davies (16)
Hampstead School

TIGER IN A STORM

There is a flash,
The sky is cracking up,
Run, run,
A piece might fall and hit me,
The shadows jump about,
There is something there,
It is after me, the unseen,
Where can I turn?
The rain is running through my fur,
Like the sweat,
The greens of the leaves are beginning to shine red,
There's a smell, a heat,
What's that I see through the bushes,
Flickering, like a cobra's tongue?
The black branches are twisting with menace,
Or is it unease?
I can feel the unease of the jungle,
Rodents are scattering before me,
They fear the lord of the jungle,
But there is a new lord, almighty,
Towering high up above even an elephant,
Cracking the sky,
Sending down fires
And spirits too.
I can feel the paranormal,
Chasing me, always behind me,
What will they do to me?
My eyes are wide, soaking up the light
And my fangs are dripping,
With hunger,
But there's no time for food,
I must run.
I must go where even I have never been before,
Where the vultures stalk,

If I am caught those vermin will peck at my corpse,
'Til I am but a skeleton, a memory,
There is a wind drying my fur,
A beautiful ray of light bursts through,
A hole in the darkness,
The darkness is passing,
I have beaten the enemy,
The flame of my fur shines once again.

Arun Sethi (14)
Hampstead School

SURPRISE!

Jolting through the bushes
A wild, savage beast

Started and shaken
Hastily he goes.

Through the hail
The blizzard and rain

His reverberating pulse
Thudding loudly

Above the enormous
Roars of thunder.

Over rustling bushes
Under swaying branches

He bounds and pounces
Then ducks and cowers

He is not the hunter.
He is the hunted.

Keara Stewart (14)
Hampstead School

THROUGH THE LONG JUNGLE GRASS

Thunder rolled across the land,
Lightning flashed across the sky,
Rain poured down,
Down from above,
As the tiger stalked,
Through the long jungle grass.

The forest fire raged through the grass
As it spiralled out of control.
The red, blood red,
The orange and the yellow
Destroying all that lay in its path
As the tiger stalked
Through the long jungle grass.

The tiger saw the flicker
And then he smelt the fear.
Animals around him turned and fled
But still he stood
Waiting, watching
Watching the mesmerising flames
As they flickered and danced
And still the fire continued
Through the long jungle grass.

But then the fire
Touched his golden coat
And the fear inside him
Made him turn and flee
A mad race against the fire
Who would win? Who would die?
As he ran for his life
Through the long jungle grass.

Abigail Hay (14)
Hampstead School

BODY IN THE BOG IN 1940

Ancient, crumbling bones;
Wrinkled, loose skin
Like a rotten apple;
The body in a bent position,
Bumps and ditches all over his face;
Unrecognisable with its decaying features.
He's moulded into clammy peat,
As warm as a kitten snuggled on a soft sofa,
But isolated and lonely.
Shrivelled skin bare to the damp soil
Except for a belt and hat.

His 2000 year old memory still recalls the stubbly rope tightening
Around his neck,
A frantic struggle,
Gasping for air;
Watching goggle eyed as the two murderers
Pull the rope,
His mouth wide open
In a silent plea for help;
Letting Mother Earth enter and take him to the world of the dead.

In his confused head, he knows not of the disturbance yet to come:
The moon light will shine through his earthy coffin,
Two aliens with shiny objects and wooden handles will stare.
He will be tampered with, exploited and will enter a new world.
What's more,
Allegations and other nonsense written.
Only he will know his history.

Ollie Haydon-Mulligan (13)
Haverstock School

Millennium Experience

Let's face it the millennium is near
Or shall I say millennium fear is here.
As some people say enjoyment and laughter is not for such a year
for the end is here.
Well I think that's not true
This is a time to have fun and see smiles on people's faces.
People are laughing at the things they see, they see everything
except unhappy faces.
I wonder why they call this bug a Millennium Bug, is it
because of an unknown creature lurking its way into
computers features? So now they get this illness a very hard
illness, the computers are down, lying on the ground
watching this miserable game being played messing with
business and finance.
Havoc is everywhere nothing can be done. But hey! None of this
can happen this is something I think might happen!
Look at the good side of the coming millennium, the
Millennium Dome is open, where you see what you can really be.
Millenniums are not something to be dealt with but something to
be faced with. I am happy of seeing such days were children are
playing with the New Years excitement. This poem was so long that
the millennium is here now so no time to rush and buy all the
celebration but see the millennium your way. Now that's a
millennium experience.

Hamed Shojanoori (13)
Kingsbury High School

The Millennium

The millennium is on its way,
We celebrate on that supreme day.
There are only seventy nine days till the time
I think this poem will really rhyme.
The Millennium Bug will come,
But I think it's really dumb.
People will go to the Millennium Dome.
I would rather stay at home.
Some people think the millennium is bad
But I think they're really mad.
People think the world's going to end
But I think the beginning of the millennium will be like a trend.
I think the millennium is cool
Especially when there are a new set of rules.

Harry Wu (12)
Kingsbury High School

The Millennium

The millennium is close, it's near,
So close that anyone would fear,
Some souvenirs they would keep
And later they would peek.
People say the millennium is bad,
But I think they're all gone mad.
The Millennium Bug is a virus,
But the computer can't read the thousands,
People say that World War 3 would start,
But then everything would turn around.

Himal Hirani (12)
Kingsbury High School

COOL CAT

Well I'm a cat with nine
And I am in my prime.
I'm a cool cat and I am feline fine.
I'm slowly swayly strolling down the street
In my white slipper feet.
Yeah! All the lady cats are looking because I've got style
Yep! I also have the best cool smile.
I am going to cross the street to collect my chicken treat,
Because it's 3 o'clock and it's time to eat.
I can see a cat with grace,
She has a very cute face.
But because I am on my own
I like to be alone.
I am just a small swinging, cute, rollin, strollin stone;
But it's her lucky day,
I'm going to pass her way.
I look in the mirror and see a twinkling eye.
I am going to cross the street
She better not be too shy.
What's that I see?
Coming straight at me.
It's a crazy driver trying to make me flee.

Just to let him know,
I look up very slow.
To show him that I don't go any faster,
Than I really wanna go,
Well I'm a cat with eight,
I guess he couldn't wait,
But I'm looking good and feline great.

Dipal Patel (12)
Kingsbury High School

The Cycle

One day the world will be at peace,
One day the world will be anti-violent
One day the world will be clean
One day the world will be gone!

Death, misery, destruction is this
What the world has come to
A boy lays still with no life in him at all
Once again a soul has been taken by the cycle.

People wonder what has happened?
People wonder what has been made?
A world which God built for humans to live in
But yet it was made into hell, not by animals,
Not my Mother Nature but by us,
The sky is not blue but is filled with hatred with each other,
The ground is not brown but is black
Filled with death
This is what we have made.

Life is gone, life is finished
With no hope and love
People wonder through the street scared of what might happen
Is this what the world has come to?
Now the millennium is coming,
With new hope and life,
We wait for this world to change
We hope we can walk with no fear
And walk with pride.
We hope that the next 1000 years is what
God intended to do.

Rikesh Jani (12)
Kingsbury High School

TAZ WOMAN

Taz woman
Is my worst dinner lady
She acts like a baby
She's got a big belly
And she's very smelly.

Taz woman
Eats out of the bin
And she's not slim
She eats half cooked chilli
And that makes her silly.

Taz woman
Eats off the floor
And bashes on the door
She tries to sing
But can't read or anything.

Taz woman
Can't afford good silk
Or even expired milk
She spends lots of money
And she thinks it's funny.

Taz woman
Is bad luck
And her feet look like ducks
By no one though she was admired
Which is what got her fired.

Kavita Joshi (12)
Kingsbury High School

HOW THE WORLD BEGAN?

Once the world was a speck of dust
As it grew, water and land were made.
First dinosaurs, then cavemen, now us.
What will the world come to?
There was World War one then two.
What will the people think of us as we destroy
the world by polluting the rivers and seas and the world?
Will there be a year 2000? Just think will younger children
Then us see the world?
Just think what the world will come to next.
Nature destroying the world by hurricanes and
Earthquakes will this ever end?
As we have in the past few months the horrific
Disasters as people die.
Poorer countries like Ethiopia, people with diseases
And with no good. Imagine, what the
World will be like next?

Vishaal Sachania (13)
Kingsbury High School

UNDERWATER

Sharks, seals, crabs, jellyfish, coral,
Dolphins,
Turtles, seaweed, sea horses, whales,
Star fish and penguins,
Are all part of sea life.
Some have teeth as sharp as a knife
Some are cute and cuddly
But some are really ugly.
Some sting, some bite,
Some don't eat people, but some might!

Anita Advani (13)
Kingsbury High School

THE MILLENNIUM POEM

The Millennium Dome is big and round
You can fit two giants big and round
The Millennium Bug is a small virus
Which can give an illness to your computer.
The 21st century is going to be cool
Which is going to be very cold.
The computers are back to life
Which can help you the rest of your life
The third world war is going to start
With a nuclear bomb doing a big fart.
Millions of people are going to die
Going to heaven crying that they died
Adolph Hitler is laughing his head off
Bombing the countries which are poor
It's the end of the world
Because the aliens are coming
Everyone's crying saying goodbye to the world!

On Doomsday - Goodbye!

Vikash Vekaria (12)
Kingsbury High School

I WISH, DO YOU?

I wish I could fly,
No one in my way,
High, high in the sky
A peaceful time to think and pray.

I wish I could read minds,
Always wondering what I'd find
Are they really what they seem?
Or is it just a dream?

Where do we go when we die?
I wish I knew for sure,
Up above,
Down below,
No one really knows.

You think you know a lot,
But do you?
Are you right?
Are you wrong?
I wish, I wish, I knew.

So I wish, do you?

Jaydene Sacha Harper (13)
Kingsbury High School

MILLENNIUM

The millennium is coming,
Some people are happy, some people sad,
Some people even going mad,
Will the world end?
Will there be a war?
Is it time for a new life?
People asking different questions.
Should I even give a mention?
Help me, help me,
I'm stuck in this hectic schedule of life.
Is there even a meaning of life?
Oh, I don't know, you have to help me
Before it's too late.
The millennium is coming soon,
What will you do?

Para Manko (13)
Kingsbury High School

WAR OR PEACE?

The millennium is here,
It's the best time of year,
There are parties and dancing,
Everyone is cheering,
People count 10, 9, 8, 7, 6, 5, 4, 3, 2, 1
Doom!
The world is silent,
There's no cheering or dancing,
The rumours were true,
There's nothing we can do,
The world is over,
The year 2000 is over,
It was here and now is gone,
It went when everyone said 1,
10, 9, 8, 7, 6, 5, 4, 3, 2, 1, gone.

Stephanie Johnson (12)
Kingsbury High School

THE MILLENNIUM POEM

Well, you're probably wondering what's going to happen
on the first of January, exactly at twelve o'clock in the millennium.
Well, everybody has been waiting for the big day to come,
well now it's your big chance, the millennium has arrived.
You're probably planning what you're going to do in the millennium
Well whatever you do be safe and don't do anything silly.
People are planning to go and visit outer space, very strange!
Well, anyway, I hope you have a wonderful millennium
and a great future.

Urmila Kerai (12)
Kingsbury High School

CHANDNI HIRANI

Chandni Hirani wears a hood,
With hair as black as ebony wood.
She has eyes as big as eggs
A cricket bat is surely not her leg?

She has a face as round as a pie,
She does something bad and says a big lie.
She wears different coloured capes,
But her toes are like grapes.

Her thighs are as wide as a football
She wishes to have a party in the Greenford Hall.
When the teacher's not there, she beats a boy
She's got a secret, she admires Roy.

The girl's belly button is like a cornflake,
She likes to eat a lot of cake!
Her nose is as pointed as an arrow
She likes to ride in a wheelbarrow.

When she walks down the corridor it looks
Like she's got all the power,
But sometimes she can be as sweet as a flower,
Well that's all about Chandni
The girl with a surname Hirani.

Poonam Mepani (12)
Kingsbury High School

THE WITCHES OF THE NIGHT

Witches love black
Black is the colour of the night
Black is the opposite of white
Witches love black.

They have cats
And black hats
They have broomsticks that can fly
Witches love black.

Witches have long nails that are black
Witches have spotty faces that are green
Witches have black cloaks
Witches love black.

Black is the colour of suits
Which people wear to funerals
Black is the colour of ashes
Witches love black.

The darkest cloud is black
The sky is black when there is a thunderstorm
Black can cover up any other colour
Witches love black.

Paints are black
Colours of the walls are black
Everywhere you look you can see black
Witches love black.

Witches eyes are always black
You would never see another colour but black
Witches love black.

Witches don't like other colours,
But witches only love black.

Krishma Vaghela (12)
Kingsbury High School

THE MILLENNIUM 2000

The millennium 2000 has come to stay,
Now I am going to rule the world.
I'll soon be king, of the country,
Working through the beads on my pearls.
Everybody's here and cheering my name,
To cut the ribbon of the new library.
The Millennium Bug is spreading,
Through thousands of computers slowly.
A new computer is built and lots of people are getting them,
Find a seat and sit on it, otherwise you won't be able to see.
The people of the government have made a new law,
People who prank telephone calls will be sentenced
10 years in hard labour.
There has been a parade and has been celebrated,
Just can't wait till I get a new computer.
People are getting worried about an earthquake,
It is my job to tell them to relax.
I would have to do the housework every day,
If I wanted anything in the world.
Now the millennium's gone, it's time to celebrate,
The new year has come and it's time to forget all
The bad memories.

Mohsin Hussain (12)
Kingsbury High School

MY LOVE FOR JANE

At ten I loved Jane
But I was frightened to say
And I suffered frustration
Throughout the school day.
I kicked at her ankles, it rankled and
Brought attention, but not the affection
I fought the strengths of my feelings,
I couldn't admit, out of my weakness I acted a git.

Then John appeared in a neighbouring seat
He said that her writing was lovely and neat
And that she really had lovely feet
And then she became chummy,
It churned up my tummy.

Back at the bungalow lacking delight
I blurted the hurting at dinner one night
I said how I loved her and it wasn't right
And at that moment I lost my heart
For the girl I loved with a vital part.

Dumisani Chirwa (13)
St Mary's CE High School, Downage

MIRROR

When we look in the mirror
Me and my friend
Her eyes are as black as a raven's wing and
My eyes are as blue as a sapphire's ring.

When we look in the mirror
Me and my friend
Her hair is curly, long and black
And my hair is short, straight and blonde.

When we look in the mirror
Me and my friend
She is as tall as a ladder and
I am as small as a stool.

When we look in the mirror
Me and my friend
We feel we are the same, same as can be,
Even though she is black and I am white,
We feel like sisters, she and me.

Zeodora Dujmovic (13)
St Mary's CE High School, Downage

AMAZING LIGHT

When I let the right ones out, I let them out, but
Then I let the wrong ones in.
I once had an angel
Who took me through my sins.
There were times in my life
When I was going insane,
Round and round
I just couldn't get out of the pain.
Then I lost my grip and fell to the floor.
I thought I could leave,
But I couldn't find the door.
I was so sick of living a lie,
I thought I was going to die.
It's amazing when that moment arrives,
When you know you're gonna be alright.
It's a wonderful feeling 'cause yet again
You can see that amazing light.

Rachel Carmichael (13)
St Mary's CE High School, Downage

MY BEDROOM

My bedroom's always in a mess,
Because I never tidy it I guess,
That day I found chocolate all over my dress,
If only life could have less stress!

Papers, pens, books and pencils,
Under the bed, all over the floor
And even behind my brown wooden door,
One day I found a swarm of dust all
Over the window sill,
If only my room would be tidy with
Just a magic pill.

When my family members walk into my room,
They walk straight out,
But I know why, because it smells of trout.

Mum tells me off for being messy,
But I am famous at being fussy,
Sometimes it is a bit of a battle,
But my excuse is I am still little.

Lavina Suthenthiran
St Mary's CE High School, Downage

ENVY ME NOT

Don't be jealous of the way I look
It's not my fault that you cannot cook
And it's not my fault why you haven't
Got my looks!

Don't blame me that you always cry,
It's not my fault that you are very shy,
Don't blame me or envy me
You are you and I am I.

Why try to act like me, 'cause it don't come over,
Be yourself, not someone else.
There's no need to argue with the teacher,
Because it don't make friends, it just ruins your future.
Don't act like a fool, be yourself and play it cool.

Stop it, stop doing that,
I've got my trends and you've got yours,
All you have to do is ask and we can be friends.

But please, please don't envy me.

Loretta King (12)
St Mary's CE High School, Downage

THE STRAY CAT

The stray lonely cat walks outside
He looks at me with his big green eyes.
He has no owner or home
He just sits there
Sad and alone.

It's cold and damp
Where he sits beneath the tree
He walks down the street
He wakes everyone up
Especially me.

No one knows where he comes from
He hardly comes into sight
He just sits there miaowing
Keeping me up half the night.
His fur is white like fresh bright snow.
What is his name? Nobody knows.

Balaal Malik (12)
St Mary's CE High School, Downage

WHAT AM I?

I fly in the sky
As shy as a fly.

I sing in the trees high above
As though as a dove.

I make my nest out of mud and leaves.
I am really pleased.

What do you think I ought to be?
I'll clap my wings and count to three.
Tell me how before I leave.

I am a bird in the air
Do you want to be with me there?

Puneh Mohammed (12)
St Mary's CE High School, Downage

THINKING IN MY HEAD

I'm sitting in my bed
Thinking in my head,
Why are we here?

I'm sitting in my bed
Thinking in my head,
Do I really care?

I'm sitting in my bed
Thinking in my head,
Is this a nightmare?

Shamaine Boyce (13)
St Mary's CE High School, Downage

In The Future

In the future things will be great,
Virtual reality and simulation,
Every country, every nation,
All running in the human race.

Hover cars will be great,
All of creation,
Animals too,
Will feel the future,
Turn on turn.

Schools improved to perfection,
No ills or germs or infection,
A peaceful nation
And also a peaceful world.

George Johnston (11)
St Mary's CE High School, Downage

The Sea

The sea is a place with no mercy,
No care and no love except for Mother Nature,
Who is the bearer of the sea and vast creatures
That live in the sea.
The sea and its big rough waves look out for
Nobody and nobody looks out for them.
They are tender in a way but untrustworthy with a life.
The sea sweeps across islands with its tsunamis,
Taking life after life until it is satisfied that every
Living thing is devastated.
Your life cannot depend on the sea but can depend on fish.
The sea, the sea, the sea what a wondrous place.

Anthony Karanu Kabuba (14)
St Mary's CE High School, Downage

SCHOOLS!

School is a place of learning, students in
Their English class reading and writing.

In their science class with equipment
Out and a Bunsen burner, burning.

With some students who don't want the
Bell to go after school
And some students who can't wait for the
Bell to go so they can play a game of pool.

Students fighting in the lunch queue
Hungry for food and drink.

Outside in the playground choosing
Their favourite numbers and colours
Which turned out to be three and pink.

Students come home to do a lot
Of homework which some students
Don't even try.

And when they come the next day
To give in their homework,
They try to explain and make
Up silly things which turn out
To be lies.

Janine Wright (13)
St Mary's CE High School, Downage

A Tribute To Owen Hart

The location was Kansas City Missouri,
The date was Sunday twenty-seventh May,
For all of us watching on TV,
To watch a death caused great pain.

He was the younger brother of the famous Bret,
He was born into a wrestling family,
It was what he wanted to do,
For him to die for it showed his commitment.

It was an Ordinary World Wrestling Federation Pay-Per-View,
It was named 'Over the Edge'
The moment that cable disconnected,
Owen plunged to his death.

He fell ninety feet,
Onto bare concrete,
When they lifted him out of the arena,
Not one of us suspected he would die.

Owen wanted to entertain the fans,
He was technically gifted,
He started his career as the Blue Blazer,
The Blue Blazer ended his life.

Owen, all wrestling fans are going to miss you,
We all know the pain your family is feeling,
We all respect your work,
God Bless you, Owen.

David Bell-Gam (13)
St Mary's CE High School, Downage

SCHOOL

7 am bleep, bleep, bleep,
The alarm's going off
All I want to do is sleep.

'Get up, get up'
I hear Mum call
'It's time for you to go to school.'

Standing at the bus stop in the
Freezing cold rain
6 hours to go
Before I'm back home again.

German, History,
Geography and Tech
I've forgotten my History book
Oh Heck!

The lunch queue
Is a mile long,
Everybody pushes and shouts,
I hope I get there in time
Before the food runs out.

Period five is History
Geography follows that
Then it's off to the bus stop
Where we sit and chat.

Back through the doors of
Home, sweet home.
Dinner, TV and a game
Then it's time for homework
It's enough to drive you
Insane!

Sarah J Shore (13)
St Mary's CE High School, Downage

FLOWING IDEAS

The darkness of night,
The light of day,
The rush of ideas.

All these ideas rushing through my head
For a poem I do not dread
What subject should I do?

The lion king of the jungle
The tigers strong as steel
Crikey! What shall I do?

The smell of mint or,
The cinema?
Many, many ideas.

You see how much trouble
This is causing me?
I might as well give up! You see?

Jason Hardman (11)
St Mary's CE High School, Downage

LOVE

Love is a flower on a tree,
As bright as it can be,
Love's not very far
Because it lights like a star.

You can see hearts banging from the wall
Heart's the colour red which is the
Best of them all,
Go fly and spread your wings,
Go, go fly in the sky and also sing.

Shaz Forozan (12)
St Mary's CE High School, Downage

THE WOLFPACK RAP

Wolfpack back cause of mass destruction
Place to see cause of bad eruption
What you got to see is no domination
Way to enter is the new dimension.

So don't turn your back on the wolfpack.

Don't think you're great and get in the way of the wolfpack
Cause they come bursting out and take you out
From here to Singapore.

So don't turn your back on the wolfpack.

Mathararaj Nithianantharajah (13)
St Mary's CE High School, Downage

STONE-COLD STEVE AUSTIN

S tunning performances always
T alking about all the bad sportsman, he beat in the past
O n the way to the top
N ever failing an attempt
E ager to defeat the dark side.

C ommitted to his duties
O ver excited crowd as he approaches the ring
L eaving his opponents helpless
D ominating the stone cold stunner - 3 seconds before he
                              wins the gold and heart of young fans.

Patrick Hickey (12)
St Mary's CE High School, Downage

MAGIC MIRRORS

The magical maze we enter through,
Are full of unknown screens.
Flashing gleams, sparkles and twinkles,
Coming in through the speed of light,
Coming so your mystery will never end.

What you see are lives, confusing sights.
Glowing on your double crossing screens.
Once you're in you,
May never get out.
Your heart will beat but,
You will still be lost in,
The world which was never found.

Angles of light will show your way
But eternity mirrors,
Will lose your game.

Suddenly you catch,
A sight of corridors.
But which one is it,
You will never know.

Behind the vision under,
The puzzled world of tricks.
Lies freedom, paradise, so
Why not take a risk of,
Turning left or right.

Harsha Patel (12)
St Mary's CE High School, Downage

GUILTY CONSCIENCE

Run away,
Run away,
I will still find you,
There is nowhere to hide,
Nowhere to run,
I will still find you.

Hide in the forest,
Hide by the river,
Hide in the sewers,
I will still find you.

Run to London,
Run to France,
Run to Italy,
I will still find you.

Nowhere to hide,
Nowhere to run,
I am your guilty conscience,
You are stuck with me.

Olaolu Oloyede (12)
St Mary's CE High School, Downage

THE SUN

A flaming, fiery furnace,
Torturing the sky,
Within its hot and fiery depths,
No planes or aircraft can fly.

The centre of the galaxy,
A seething, boiling globe of gas,
It has nine planets that are family
Of this gigantic mass.

A source of light and heat to us,
This ball of fire proclaims,
The king of all things . . .
The sun carries out its reign.

We praise the sun glorious,
For if it was not there,
Everything that's light would be dark
And night would reign again.

Sam Layton (11)
St Mary's CE High School, Downage

BATTERSEA DOG HOME

As I walked round Battersea Dog Home
I thought 'Which one shall I pick?
I want one I can take to the park,
And throw him a ball or a stick.'

There were hundreds of pleading eyes,
Staring at me through the cages.
'I want one I can take to the shop
And wait there for ages and ages.'

I walked for ages and I finally found
A very pretty Basset hound.
I was going to take him until I saw
A very friendly Labrador.

I suddenly saw a Jack Russell.
Until I saw the muzzle.
I turned round and there I saw,
A bearded collie.
She was very sweet and her name was Mollie.

Katie Stimson (12)
St Mary's CE High School, Downage

SCHOOL

The bell goes at twenty to nine
And all the children rush into line.
They look like blue bees,
Swarming over warm sticky honey.
They leave the playground
Class by class
Until the very last.
The playground is left,
Quiet and still,
Just like when you've
Taken a sleeping pill.
Up in the classrooms,
Registers are taken and,
Questions are asked.
Good kids sit quietly,
Naughty ones being let off lightly.
'Please class, do pay attention,
Or I'll have to give you a detention.'
Not wanting to miss
The bus home,
We all sit up straight,
With a slight moan.

Jade Cottrell (12)
St Mary's CE High School, Downage

BEST FRIEND

I hope that our friendship will never end,
Too young to understand but now you're my best friend,
When my world crashes and my world stops,
I know you'll be there as from the start.

Because you mean the world to me,
Thanks for being a great friend to me,
You're the closest one to me,
I surrender all to thee,
I want the whole wide world to see,
That you are and will always be my best friend.

Simon Sullivan (11)
St Mary's CE High School, Downage

MY INVISIBLE FRIEND

No one believes me, but she's there, (she is)
She's with me all the time, (she is)
I know everything about her, (I do)
Her favourite flavour's lime. (Yuk)

My mother thinks it's just a phase, (mean Mum)
She doesn't understand, (no)
My horrible big brother, Mike (he's mean)
Thinks I'm in another land. (I'm not)

But I know she's there, I know it, (I do)
She's with me every day, (she is)
Mum asked me what she looks like, (Oh dear)
I didn't know what to say. (Uh, uh)

I mean, I can't really see her, (no)
I just know she's there, (I do)
My dad said that I'm silly (he did)
But he just doesn't care. (Not at all)

One day I know she'll leave me, (she will)
Go to another girl, (she will)
But it won't be the same without her, (it won't)
'I'm really going to miss you, Pearl.' (Bye bye)

Christina McNamara (12)
St Mary's CE High School, Downage

THE MOON

When I used to be a child,
I thought the moon was a cradle,
And my grandma was in there
Waiting to give me a kiss and a cuddle.

I used to think the new moon
Was a banana.
And the full moon was
A big cream cake.

When I was a child
I saw the moon how
I wanted to see it,
Never the real moon.

Now I see the real moon
It's the big and
Shiny moon,
And only the moon.

Payal Jolapara (12)
St Mary's CE High School, Downage

MY LIFE

This is my life
I have only one wife
Two children I did bear
Who just glare and stare
I go to the pub at night
And can't miss one fight
So this is the life which
I share with my wife.

Victor Matovu (11)
St Mary's CE High School, Downage

TROY'S INVASION

There . . .
at midnight,
The snoring drowned out.
By the cold,
sleepless night.
The wooden horse waits,
in the massive kingdom.
Inside the gift,
Are
Ghostly soldiers.
Ckr Ckrrrrrr Ckrr.
What's that?
Oh no!
It's that door,
It's opening.
Soldiers are creeping out.
The light is absent,
The battle sets about,
Executed heads start to appear,
At the end,
Take,
One big blow,
Troy is now dust.

Nilam Patel (13)
St Mary's CE High School, Downage

LOVE

Love is romantic,
Love is always passionate,
Love is between two.

Pasindu Silva (13)
St Mary's CE High School, Downage

THE DAY TODAY

The day today is the worst of the days,
it's the day that we start back at school.

But when you're at school you have to
be cool, but some just play the fool!

Lunchtime's OK when we go out to play . . .
except when it rains and the children complain
as we squeeze ourselves into the gym.

At the end of the day full of work,
food and play, we all pack away . . .
     And go home!

James Alexander Pettican (12)
St Mary's CE High School, Downage

SECRET PLACE

In a secret box,
In a secret room,
In a secret attic,
Up the secret stairs,
In a secret hall,
In a secret house,
On a secret road,
In a secret town,
In a secret book,
With a secret key,
Which unlocks a secret door,
Which leads to a secret tomb,
Where the secret mummy goes.
     'Boo!'

Ruth Matsunaga (12)
St Mary's CE High School, Downage

MY BAD DAY

When I woke up in the morning, I hit my head hard,
Walked down the stairs, (I'm surprised I didn't fall)
Got my breakfast, dropped my plate,
Grabbed my books, got out of the door,
I thought I was safe now.

Went round the corner,
Buckled on the pavement
Jumped on the bus, it was so squashy,
My stop came, I ran out of the bus.

Someone asked me for the time,
'8:40' I replied. Oh no, I'm late
Legged it the whole way, saw the caretaker, he said
'Why are you here on a Saturday morning?'
Oh no I really am having a bad day.

Forum Shah (12)
St Mary's CE High School, Downage

FOOTBALL

'Foul, yellow card, send him off.'
'Oh what a fun day it's going to be.'
Out in cold weather.
Time for something to eat at half-time.
Balls flying from place to place
'And he scores.'
Loud moans and groans
Laughs and cries at the end of the day.

Dionne Benjamin (12)
St Mary's CE High School, Downage

THE MONTHS OF THE YEAR

January brings the new year,
But do not drink too much beer.

February is usually a happy time,
For those who are with their Valentines.

March brings your mother presents,
But make sure it is pleasant.

April brings the Easter bunny,
I hope you get lots of money.

May brings May Day,
I hope you have a lovely day.

June brings Father's Day,
Let's all shout 'Hooray.'

July brings the end of school,
The holidays are going to be really cool.

August brings summertime,
Mix lemonade with lime.

September, we go back to school,
Be there, unless you're a fool.

October brings photograph day,
Time to get your parents to pay.

November is when autumn's gone,
Time to get your mittens on.

December brings the winter snow
And Father Christmas says 'Ho ho ho.'

Faye Blair (13)
St Mary's CE High School, Downage

My Family

My family is different in a special way,
'Do this! Do that!' is all my mum seems to say.
She's brilliant considering everything she does for me,
Like clean the house and make my tea.

My dad sometimes gets home late at night,
But when I see him I am glad,
Even though he sometimes gets quite mad.

My brother and I argue a lot,
But whatever it's about,
We always sort it out.
You should see us when we're getting on well,
It is swell.

Soléne Bhagwanani (12)
St Mary's CE High School, Downage

Titanic

The Titanic was a notorious boat
Which was generally regarded to stay ever afloat.
It was flagship of the *White Star Line*
This ship was clean and fine.

The Titanic was the largest ship of its day
The chrome work shone as it passed the bay
The captain must have been very skilled
Too bad he was later killed.

The Titanic weighed 46,000 tons
Fully laden with two battle guns
It had 50 lifeboats on its deck
It was soon to be known that it would be a total wreck.

Ricardo Reittie (12)
St Mary's CE High School, Downage

MONEY ISN'T EVERYTHING

Money isn't everything,
it cannot bring you joy.
It can only bring you simple things,
like stereos and toys.
But what about the times,
When you are alone and down?
Money cannot help you,
it just sits on the ground.
But what about a friend,
that can make you laugh and sing.
And when all your friends are gone,
you think of the fun they bring.
Just think of a friend
And how they help out.
And how they talk to you about problems,
you know what I'm on about.
What about a friend,
who can help you carry on?
The one that you can learn from,
to teach you right and wrong.
So don't forget your friends,
when you have money and fame.
Or else next time you need a friend,
your life won't be the same.

Antonio Corbin (12)
St Mary's CE High School, Downage

LOOK ALIKES

The good twin is as good as gold
She's not outgoing, but she's bold.
She does her homework right on time
Her maths makes sense,
Her poems rhyme.

The bad twin mostly stays in trouble,
She's so unlike her clever double
She doesn't even know what a poem is
How can that be
When her sister's a wiz?

How could there be two different girls
Who look so much the same?
Their personalities are opposites,
They've been told
Again and again.

One turns pages in books,
While the other acts all vain.
She cares too much about her looks,
She's a daredevil
With no shame.

Jessica Ward (12)
St Mary's CE High School, Downage

OH NO! HIGH SCHOOL

The day before High School,
I was feeling very glum
'Oh no! High School,' I said,
'Yes,' said Mum.
The day before High School,
All I did was cry
Scared, nervous, shaking
Wanting to die.
The day before High School,
I was wondering about the kids
Those big, tall and humungous
Making fun of me.
Those who looked like giants,
Running in gangs of four,
Compared to them I was an ant
Who was little, alone and had no more
'Don't worry!' Mum said,
'There are others in your place
As the days will go past
You have nothing to worry about.'
The day before High School
I was worried sick about being bullied.
'You won't!' said my mum
What are teachers for?
'I will get lots of homework' I said
'So,' said my mum
'I won't have time to finish it.'
'How do you know that for sure?'
The hours before High School,
I couldn't even sleep
All I did was toss and turn
My mum was mad at me.

When the day finally arrived,
I had gone all red
I couldn't even sleep
My mum pulled me out of bed.
After I came back from High School,
This is what I said
'Oh yes! High School'
'Yes,' said Dad.

Prachi Mesvani (12)
St Mary's CE High School, Downage

WATERFALLS OF LIFE

Waterfalls are magic, didn't you know?
They hold all of life's answers,
Every person has his own waterfall,
They know you, sense you and live your life.
When you're happy it will splash with joy,
It will jump around and run over the hills,
It will make a soft spray as it hits the water
And dance around like a little kid.
When you're sad it will show,
The wall will wither thin and show bare rock,
There are only tiny droplets falling like tears from your eyes,
Everything is still and quiet.
When you're angry nothing will calm it.
It will race and splash and roar like a storm at sea,
It will wash away anything it touches with a great force,
Nothing is safe.
As you change your moods it changes its path,
It rushes along overflowing with emotions,
The magic will sprinkle for ever over your life,
As you wish and dream of your waterfall.

Samantha Burcher (13)
St Mary's CE High School, Downage

FRIENDSHIP

Friends are for ever
And boyfriends come and go,
Because a friend can help you out with stuff
Which boyfriends couldn't know.

A friend will know what your problem is
And comfort you night and day
Your boyfriend will pass you by, my dear,
But a friend is here to stay!

Sabina McCulloch (12)
St Mary's CE High School, Downage

WHY?

Why?
Why are there falling, fluttering flies?
Why are there gorgeous, greeny, grassy, guys?
Why are there beautiful, bright blue skies?

Why?
Why do people say harmful, horrible goodbyes?
Why do people say nasty, neglectful lies?
Why do people shamefully die?
Why?

Yasmin Putz (13)
St Mary's CE High School, Downage

TOUCHED BY AN ANGEL'S LIGHT

I was asleep in my bed,
All calm and cosy,
Where everything was rosy.

A flash of light appeared in the night,
I shielded my eyes from the brilliant sight,
At the end of my bed and dressed in white,
An angel took to flight.

I squinted hard to see,
As I heard a tuneful sound,
I felt a sense of wonder,
As she floated softly around.

As she sang, how sweet her tune,
She floated up towards the moon,
I watched her light fade too soon.

Now she was gone,
I felt alone.

I looked up to the sky
And there was a sign,
A star shining brightly,
A symbol of love, peace and harmony.

Catharine Bishop (13)
St Mary's CE High School, Downage

POKÉMON

Pokémon is good,
Pikachu is the cutest,
Gotta catch 'em all.

Christopher Fennelly (13)
St Mary's CE High School, Downage

INDIA'S FREEDOM

The story of India's freedom,
I am going to tell you;
Tonnes of blood were shed,
Just to gain freedom for you.
Thousands of families were destroyed,
Thousands of men were killed;
Numbers of houses were set on fire,
Numerous graves were built.
Sons were dead and old and sick were left alone,
But still they were proud of their children
Who fought for their country's throne.
Many leaders were put into jail,
The reason they had revolted;
The police killed them with their guns,
When the commoners protested.
People were sad but were sure of one thing,
That one day India would be free and again
Happy like a freshly grown tree.
At last on 15th August 1947
The British had to say goodbye.
And thus the tricolour rose
High in the sky.

Sandhya Ahuja (12)
St Mary's CE High School, Downage

A TRUE FRIEND

A true friend stands by you,
Like a fox to its cubs.

A true friend is warm and loving,
Like a wood fire on a cold winter's day.

A true friend picks you up when you're down,
Like a helping hand invisible to the world.

A true friend is always there for you
Like a mother and a father.

A true friend is a true blessing.

Gabrielle Brewster (13)
St Mary's CE High School, Downage

WHAT A CAT!

I know a cat
who's brown and black,
as quick as a flash,
does not wait to chat.

Always getting stuck up trees,
we like chocolate, she likes cheese,
you stroke her head, she licks your knees,
what a cat, full of fleas.

I open the door,
she's on the fence,
'Get down to the floor'
I shout with all my strength.

My cat is not like that,
never does she mess the mat,
Kittie's her name, the perfect cat.

I know a cat
who's brown and black,
as quick as a flash,
does not wait to chat.

Esha Massand (13)
St Mary's CE High School, Downage

THE UNDERGROUND GNOMES

We are always sure about the day,
but when we think about it what
mysteries unfold in the night.
While we are sleeping who knows
what strange things are happening?
There is one thing even scientists can't unfold.
This mystery is the underground gnomes.
These creatures ascended from the north
and only come out at night,
when all living souls are sleeping.
They go around quietly collecting food for their families.
They also go around equalising,
they listen to anyone who makes a wish
and equalises with the person who did the deed,
and pays him back in a gruesome way.
Not only that but they keep the
Remains!

Michael Campbell (13)
St Mary's CE High School, Downage

MY FAMILY THE GALAXY

The sun is my mother because she's the centre of our world
The moon is my father because he guides us home
The stars are my brothers because they are so bright
And the planets are my sisters because they are untouched
I am the Milky Way because I complete this world
Together we are the galaxy united as one.

Onike Kanda (13)
St Mary's CE High School, Downage

Four Seasons

The sun shines after its long sleep,
a fresh feeling is in the air,
Spring is here, daffodils are rising,
butterflies are growing and birds are singing.
Summer's heat creeps up on us,
Roses are at their full bloom
children are chanting and squirrels are collecting.
Then it rains non-stop,
Summer months are over,
leaves are falling, changing colour,
Angry clouds conquer the dull skies,
the sun is nowhere to be seen,
Winter dawns up on autumn
White is the new craze,
wind, rain and snow are taking over
Winter is here but lasts just a bit longer.

Rubee Variava (13)
St Mary's CE High School, Downage

Disney

Mickey and Minnie the characteristic mice,
Full of colour and cheer and all things nice,
There's Goofy and Pluto the clumsy pair of dogs,
Running through forests and jumping over logs,
We meet Daffy and Daisy, the happy, friendly pair,
Daffy chasing Daisy as she floats in mid-air.
A family holiday for everyone to enjoy,
Meeting the characters who give us joy,
Showing tricks and there's dogs that float,
Here's Disneyland, but that's all folks!

Carianne Wylie (13)
St Mary's CE High School, Downage

Words

Words can be good or bad things,
Much more precious than diamond rings,
Words can change the way you think,
They provide the missing link,
What you say and what you do
Finds its way straight back to you
Words are a way to express your mind,
Words can be hurtful or be kind,
You can shout and you can scream
To tell other people what you mean.
Whatever your age, whatever your race,
Shout it out loud to everyone's face!
When you've got something to say
Words can be used in any way,
Use one to say something nice today!

Dilan Kanli (14)
St Mary's CE High School, Downage

A Poem About Flying!

Bzzzz went the engine,
It was really smooth.
We got off the ground
And saw all the views.

Look, there's my house,
Look, there's my dad's car,
There's my friend,
He really looks far.

I saw the hills,
I saw the sea,
I saw a farm
Which looked like my keys.

The engine stopped,
I got off the plane,
The airport came to view,
Hey, I'm in Spain!

Waqar Kasker (13)
St Mary's CE High School, Downage

THE RAIN

The rain slowly dripping on the ground,
As I see the clouds turn grey and dull,
I can hear the rain playing a piece of music,
So calm and so peaceful,
As I walk towards my doorstep,
The rain dripping down my fringe,
As I kick my foot in the puddle.
The rain getting heavier and heavier,
As the cars in the city fight like crazy.
The rain pouring down more quickly
As I can see people walking faster,
My coat all soaked and wet
As if I've just had a shower,
Then slowly, it's getting quieter,
And suddenly it has stopped,
As if nothing has just happened.

Angie Wong (13)
St Mary's CE High School, Downage

WHY DO YOU ALWAYS PICK ON ME?

They say I'm different, but they don't understand,
There's a bigger problem that's much more in demand.
You've got world hunger and not enough to eat,
There is so much poverty, yet you keep picking on me!
There are some teachers who refuse to teach
And there are grown people who can't write or read,
There are strange diseases with no cure,
There are so many doctors, but none of them are sure.
There is so much corruption and vanity,
It is easy to say there is a lot of pain
But there's no doubt about it, day in, day out,
You'll always find time to pick on me!
We have more problems than we will ever need,
There are homeless people finding food on the street,
There is drug addiction in the minds of the weak,
But you're always picking on me.
I don't understand your objectives.
I want to take you to a court of law
And win the battle, then the war,
But you always have to look back and see
Those in poverty!

Andreas Charalambous (13)
St Mary's CE High School, Downage

THE SUN

The sun is a star,
      You can see it from far,
But do not get too close,
      Or you'll end up like burnt toast.

Tunde Hazzan (14)
St Mary's CE High School, Downage

My Mum

Like a warm, cuddly teddy bear,
As soft as snow.

Like a roaring lion,
As loud as thunder.

Like a kind bird,
As gentle as a mouse.

Like a small rose,
As loving as can be.

Like a flash of lightning,
As quick as a fish.

Vidusha Vijayakumar (13)
St Mary's CE High School, Downage

No Way Out!

Where is everything?
All I can see is visions
Of the street, but then they vanish.
I call out for help, but all I hear
Is my echo calling back to me.
I run from place to place,
But I just feel I'm running
In circles, not knowing where next to go,
I feel no love, I feel no care,
Just me in a big, black, dark space,
With no way out.
Help!

Caroline Lowes (12)
St Mary's CE High School, Downage

THE HALF-PIPE FROM HELL

I was at the top of the half-pipe
With the wind in my hair,
I was scared from head to toe,
'Whoooh.' What was that?
It was a bird.

All I have to do is bend my knees
And not look down.
Okay, this was it, helmet check,
Knee pad check, elbow and wrist pads check,
I was scared. My heart pounded,
Boom, boom, boom.

Slip, Agghh! I was moving.
Why, nobody knows, I was flying.
I was soaring and then in a couple of seconds
It was all over.

Dominic Beeput (12)
St Mary's CE High School, Downage

FRIENDSHIP

F riendship is all about you and your friends,
R evealing the secrets that you've had from the past,
I ncluding the things which make them laugh,
E njoying every moment with the people you trust,
N ever knowing how long it would last,
D epending on whether your friendship is true,
S haring the things that you like doing best,
H aving a nice time, just being with them,
I n between, you have your arguments and fights,
P ure friendship is what this is all about.

Safeena Kadiri (13)
St Mary's CE High School, Downage

THAT PERSON

Who was that person?
When the wind was an absurd carnivore
Haunting the creepy trees,
The fiery moon was a bird's feather
Painting a trail as far as the eye could see.
The person's overcoat was a shady grey,
It made me stare in dismay.
The person's head and face were covered
With a unique coif-like hat,
Great technique was shown to make it.
When I saw those queer shoes,
I was struck with fear,
Webbed shoes and lumpy, mouldy-coloured legs.
Dark, senile thoughts crept into my head,
So many they could fill a keg.
Suddenly a shadow was cast upon me,
The last thing I saw on Earth was the luminous,
Blinding light shining over my eyes.
Soon I was floating upwards,
This was paradise,
I woke up with that person and its people, standing beside me,
To this moment, I wonder if I have seen this before?

Vikas Kapoor (13)
St Mary's CE High School, Downage

WEEKDAYS

Mondays are so mundane, mad, miserable and mean,
Tuesdays are so tiring, tactful, tense and tacky,
Wednesdays are so wicked, weak, wet and wretched,
Thursdays are so tender, temporary, tame and terrific,
Fridays are so fiery, fearful, formal and foul.

Umar Ahmed (12)
St Mary's CE High School, Downage

THE SEA AND ME

The sun is a pillar box
With pilgrims looking through.
People in Iceland, people in Peru.
People all over the world, looking up at the sun
From the smallest fly to the biggest nun.
The shapeless object that we call the sun
Is really a ball of fire,
Hanging over the sea, a giant flare from a gun.
It's great to be at the seaside,
To have a picnic on the shore,
Seeing the loony waves go high,
Willing them to reach the sky.
I just stayed with the lonesome sea,
How lonely it looked to me,
Then the moon came into view,
A soft white, round satsuma,
Filled with yellow sand,
Spinning around like a satellite,
Ignorant and bright,
Like ice on frozen water.

Carley Coles (13)
St Mary's CE High School, Downage

SCHOOL

School can be fun when it's time to dine,
Playing in the sun can also be fine,
It can be boring with teachers going on like preachers,
Then you get detention until you pay attention.

Kelvin Gichohi (13)
St Mary's CE High School, Downage

I Would Love To Be...

I would love to be a snowman,
When winter comes around,
I would stay outside all day
And sit upon the ground.

I would love to be a snowman,
With a carrot for a nose
And buttons for my mouth,
laid out in a neat row.

I would love to be a snowman,
I could watch the children play,
It would make me happy
Every winter day.

I would love to be a snowman,
Instead of being me,
I'd stay outside in winter,
For the whole world to see.

Lianne Cooper-Brown (12)
St Mary's CE High School, Downage

Wrong

Don't you hate it when things go wrong,
People laugh and say you pong,
You start out right, your brain goes bong,
Oh I hate it when things go wrong.

Don't you hate it when things go wrong,
People twirl their fingers and go ding-dong,
People hit me, I am not that strong,
I so much hate it when things go wrong.

James Mackie (11)
St Mary's CE High School, Downage

TRUE LIES

It makes me cackle and laugh with glee
At what Granny used to say to me,
That when she was young there were these things called leaves
That grew on green things called trees.

On the ground there was earth and soil
And the sea was not covered in oil.
These days she goes on saying it's not fair
To pump toxic waste into the air.

Those lies sound convincing that she said
About how she could hear animals while lying in bed,
But how could she do that?
All the animals are dead.

Granny said people in her day
Had a choice what to lose,
But now in the future,
It's too late to choose.

Paul Langley (13)
St Mary's CE High School, Downage

SCHOOL DAYS

C ome for school early,
H ates homework all the time,
A round the corner I come,
R ushing to meet my friends,
L ying in my bed, do not want to get up,
E arly in the morning coming to school,
N othing for breakfast in the morning,
E arly going to the school gates.

Charlene Wright (11)
St Mary's CE High School, Downage

Animals Go Wild

The lions scared the monkeys,
While the cheetahs were acting funky,
The hyenas started to giggle
And all the worms started to wiggle,
The giraffe was tall
And the ants were small,
The termites started chewing
And all the cows started mooing,
The fly got caught in the web
While the spider went out and got wed,
The snake started to make
A T-shirt that was fake,
The bat and the cat
Ate sweets until they were fat,
This is the end of this wacky thing,
I hope you enjoyed it and made your bell ring.

Christopher Barker (11)
St Mary's CE High School, Downage

My Sister!

My sister is annoying,
Jumping up and down,
She really gets on my nerves
When she starts running around.
She jumps off my bunk bed
And scribbles on my wall,
My sister is annoying
And it's like I do not know her at all.

Leonella Dujmovic (11)
St Mary's CE High School, Downage

MONEY

I love the ads,
They're really funny,
Telling you to buy
When you've not got the money.

Get a telly,
Get a toaster,
Get a cooker,
Get a motor.

If you ain't got the money,
It's okay to borrow,
Use a bank card,
Clear it tomorrow.

It's okay to borrow,
Bank manager said,
As long as you pay me back,
And so long as you're not dead.

Watching the telly
Some rainy day,
Bill arrives,
Oh no, can't pay.

I love the ads,
They're really funny,
Telling you to buy
When you've not got the money.

Get a telly,
Get a toaster,
Get a cooker,
Get a motor.

I love the ads,
They're really funny,
Telling you to buy
When you've not got the money.

Minal Wadhia
St Mary's CE High School, Downage

I AM FROM VENUS

Mutants with big spots
remind me of my brother.

Witches on Hallowe'en,
they look just like my sister.

Unhappy thoughts
remind me of Earth.

But I am from Venus,
where people look like grown-ups at birth.

Presents at Christmas
remind me of love.

Birds flying in the sky
make me wonder what's above.

Happy thoughts keep
the world going on.

But I am from Venus
so how can I know?

Louina Ajuo (12)
St Mary's CE High School, Downage

Runaway

I'm running from everything 'live'
I'm running from my friends,
I'm running for me and only me.

People are chasing me,
I have to keep to the back streets
Hiding under canal bridges,
Sleeping on the banks.

Police are everywhere, now I can't get away,
When they ask me questions,
I don't know what to say.

You see, I don't have family,
I only have me.
I hate everybody and everybody hates me.

I'm feeling sad and lonely,
But I don't care,
All I have in me is fear.

Jerome Jefferson (12)
St Mary's CE High School, Downage

That Face

The night of wonders had finally come.
My date was here, her eyes shone like the sun at dawn.
The busiest place seemed a tranquillity for once.
The night at the cinema has broken the ice,
The night fell and the moon shone.
Her sky-blue eyes were as bright as a torch light. ·

Talk about the film, that's all we did,
Then the subjects started to change.
It soon got personal and we both stayed put,
Then the moon showed up from behind the clouds,
As my eyes locked themselves to see nothing but her face.
We closed our eyes as our souls drove us,
I knew it was time to kiss that face.

Horacio Alberto Ortega Di Gregorio (14)
St Mary's CE High School, Downage

DOGGY DAYDREAM

I have a dog, his name is Dylan,
He really is a little villain.
Sneaking from the garden
All smelly and wet,
Hiding from my mum
Because he knows what he will get.

Muddy paws all over the floor,
Leading to the kitchen door,
Gingerly he opens it wide
To find his favourite place to hide.

Up the stairs he starts to creep
Onto the bed as he falls asleep.
In his sleep he starts to dream
Of chocolate cookies and whipped cream.

He dreams of hot dogs and mustard
And steaming hot pie and custard.
As he drifts off up in the sky,
He wishes his dream will never die.

Dana Al-Omari (13)
St Mary's CE High School, Downage

NIGHT APPEARS

Night appears when darkness falls,
Night appears with spooky halls.

Night appears with dripping taps,
Night appears with meowing cats.

Night appears with noisy cars,
Night appears with twinkling stars.

Night falls with rustling trees,
Night falls with jangling keys.

But it's okay, it's my mum,
She's come home from bingo.

Chelsea Hickey (11)
St Mary's CE High School, Downage

FEELINGS

Dear my world,
Sometimes you make me laugh,
Sometimes you make me smile,
You even make me cry,
Or I might feel high,
Although one day I'll have to say goodbye,
I'll still be glad,
Because I know I'll always be high,
Looking down on you from the sky.

Sarah Griffiths (12)
St Mary's CE High School, Downage

JESS MCBETH

In the kitchen there was a mess,
This mess was made by Jess McBeth.
Jess McBeth was really sad
Because she made people mad.

I really hate you Jess McBeth,
Why don't you go and buy a dress?
Jess McBeth hated school
Because she wasn't very cool.

The strange world of Jess McBeth
Is always quite a big, fat mess.

Josephine Balfour (12)
St Mary's CE High School, Downage

OUR NEW ARRIVALS

Snoring, purring, fidgeting, scratching,
My four white kittens sleep.

Yawning, stretching, moaning, wiping,
My four white kittens awake.

Sipping, purring, sucking, dribbling
My four white kittens eat.

Hiding, running, sliding, rolling,
My four white kittens play.

Snoring, purring, fidgeting, scratching,
My four white kittens sleep again.

Reshma Patel (12)
St Mary's CE High School, Downage

THE LAST ONE INTO BED . . .

The last one into bed
Has to switch off the light,
It's just the same very night,
There's a race!

I'm pulling off my shoes and socks,
He's ripping off his shirt and tie,
You've hidden his pyjamas,
Better keep your hands off mine.

No, oh no, it cannot be,
Why, oh why, does it have to be me?
No, oh no, not tonight,
Again it seems I must switch off the light.

Everyone's lying in their beds,
Nicely resting their tiresome heads,
While I have to make the sacrifice,
Towards my sad and lonely life.

'Turned off the light' I said,
Must dash now to my waiting bed!

Noises that I think I hear,
Voices that just disappear,
I'll only stand up just to say,
'Why does it have to be this way?'

Why does it always have to be me?
Why can't they never ever see?
Why for once can't they go instead
So I can rest my sleepy head?

So in the night,
We have this fight
Which seems all right,
For who is to turn off the light.

Natassa Charalambous (12)
St Mary's CE High School, Downage

THE DREAM

Alone in the world I stand,
I finally realise
That there's no way out.
I feel trapped,
What?
I am trapped
In this dark hole and nobody can hear me calling.
I hear a voice repeatedly saying
If it wasn't for my longing,
I may not have ended up here.

Suddenly, everything emerges,
I find myself on my bedroom floor,
My head and arm ache.
I can hear the switch of a light,
It's my mum who picks me up and
Tucks me back in bed.

Then I felt something.
I looked at my pillowcase
And there was a ball which
Contained a little girl in the dark.
Above her head was a sign which read:
The Dream!

Loretta Henry (12)
St Mary's CE High School, Downage

CHRISTMAS EVE TO CHRISTMAS DAY

Snow is falling
All around us,
Merry Christmas everyone!
The festival is here!

The shops are packed,
The streets are full,
Christmas Eve is almost here.

The burning, blazing fireplaces
With stockings hanging high,
The finishing touches to the Christmas tree,
Then the children say 'Good night.'

How I wish I could have that CD
Or bike, or even that car,
I hope Santa hurries quickly
With my prizes and presents galore!

I peel a few carrots,
Collect three cookies and milk,
I'm snuggled up in my cosy bed,
I just can't wait till morn!

I wake up in excitement,
Hundreds of presents on the floor,
My CD, my bike,
I don't know what else I can thank Santa for.

What is Christmas to everyone?

Is it the presents under the tree
Or to give and receive,
Or the birth of Jesus Christ, our Lord?
Why not have a guess and think?

Zara Park (12)
St Mary's CE High School, Downage

A Knight Without Armour

As time falls and night descends,
You lie awake till dreaming ends,
And the dawn breaks,
While earthly quakes are at a peaceful mend.
Fondly you bathe in greens and blues,
As the ocean trembles and the suns cruise,
But you cannot rise from this place,
Absent as the world's embrace,
For you are a knight without armour,
A king without crown,
A river without water,
A bird without song,
A hero at a glance,
Through magical lands and wind-soft hands,
You descend to bed,
And lie awake dead,
As if all your dreams just vanished.

Sharmaine Mehar Malik (15)
St Mary's CE High School, Downage

Flying The Flag!

Flying the flag for England,
Flying it high and strong,
Representing our English ways,
With all the other flags up high.
Up high in the sky for England,
Never falling down,
It stands out in its special way
It always flies high in the sky.

Darryn Davies (12)
St Mary's CE High School, Downage

THE LUNCH MONEY

I know you did it, I know it's true,
But I just can't believe it's you.
I didn't know you could do such a thing,
After all the things you say and sing.
You were meant to be my very best mate,
But now you're the person I love to hate.
It's impossible for me to forgive you,
As I know exactly what you do.
It's nasty, spiteful, cruel and mean
And I can't believe what I've just seen.
I'd like to see what you'd do
If the same thing happened to you.
I'd like to stick your head in honey . . .
As you've just stolen all my lunch money.

Christina Tseriotis (12)
St Mary's CE High School, Downage

ANGER ON MY BIRTHDAY

My birthday,
No laughter,
No presents,
No fun,
No happiness,
In fact, no one remembered.
I felt miserable, unhappy, angry and terrible,
I felt like screaming, but what's the use?
No one will understand why I'm screaming,
But I'll wait till next year and I'll see what happens,
But if this happens again, I'll write a book.

Tapiwa Agere (12)
St Mary's CE High School, Downage

SEA FEVER

I must go down to the seas again, to the lonely sea and the sky
And all I ask is a tall ship and a star to steer her by,
And the wheel's kick and the wind and the white sails shaking,
And a grey dawn breaking.

I must go down to the seas again, for the call of the running tide
Is a wild call and clearly may not be denied.
And all I ask is a windy day with the white cloud flowing
And the plunging spray and the blown spume
And the seagulls crying.

I must go down to the seas again, to the life of the gull's way
And the whale's way, where the wind's like a whetted knife,
And all I ask is a merry yarn with a laughing fellow rover,
And quiet sleep and a sweet dream,
When the long trek's over.

Alaba Badewa (12)
St Mary's CE High School, Downage

FRIENDSHIP

F orever they might be,
R ough times or tragedy,
I n the end they'll still be there, the ones you can depend on.
E veryone says friends come and go,
N o one says that's right you know.
D own comes the rain, up comes the sun, they will be
    your friends helping you along.
S o they help you do anything in return,
H ope you do, otherwise that friendship's through.
I f you have a fight with your friends,
P ut things right to keep your friendship light.

Nicole Bandoo (12)
St Mary's CE High School, Downage

ELLIE

Ellie is my dog,
She often sleeps like a log.

She is beautiful and pretty
But then again, very licky.

She waits at the top of the stairs
And then begins to glare.

With her puppy eyes
She glares at all the pies.

She takes a whiff of the air
And then continues to glare.

When you come through the door
She holds up her little, tiny paw.

Then she bashes her thumping tail
And we all start to wail.

Amy Chandler (12)
St Mary's CE High School, Downage

AT MY HOME

A welcoming smell as I walk through the door
T he TV blaring on Channel 4.

M y baby brother trying to sleep
Y asmin my sister wanting a treat.

H ot fire crackling in front of the settee
O lly the cat purring at me
M andy the dog chewing a bone
E ven Mum and Dad love it at home.

Kimberley Briggs (12)
St Mary's CE High School, Downage

GENIE

I grant you three wishes,
Oh yes, do the dishes,
No wait . . . oh genie, oh genie,
I think it's something I ate!

Three wishes, three wishes, how about some kisses,
No wait . . .
Oh genie, oh genie, pinch me, am I awake?

I've got it, I've got it, I'll stop it, I'll stop it,
No wait . . .
Oh genie, oh genie, I think I'll ask my mate!

What can I do with three wishes?
I don't want the dishes, I don't want some kisses!
Don't want to stop it,
But wait . . .
Oh genie, oh genie, I want a *date!*

Nivine Saleh (12)
St Mary's CE High School, Downage

PARENTS

Abrupt but complete and perfect,
Perfect as the dove of peace,
Peace so calm,
Calm and all so still,
Still like always you look attractive,
Attractive but still accessible,
Accessible whenever I need you,
You are my illuminated candle,
Candle oh so amazing you glow,
Glow on me forever and guide me.

Natallie Lucien (12)
St Mary's CE High School, Downage

THE YORKSHIRE RIPPER

The 'Ripper', Peter Sutcliff,
He was a murderer,
He never killed a 'he',
It was always a 'her',

He aimed for special people,
The women of the night,
Probably because they
Could never put up a fight.

He hit them with a hammer
And stabbed them with a knife,
He also used a screwdriver
To deprive them of their life.

Their only shred of evidence,
Was his size seven prints,
The police could use these
As their only hints.

He attempted twenty women,
Thirteen of whom did die,
When found by the police,
He tried a great, white lie.

He was caught for stealing number plates
From an old scrapyard
And from the rest of the world,
He was locked up and barred.

Steph Phillips (12)
St Mary's CE High School, Downage

Roy Keane's Goals

On the twelfth of August, Man Utd beat Arsenal 2-1,
Everyone was tired in the baking hot sun.
First Fredrick Ljungberg scored for Arsenal, the Gunners'
  fans went mad,
'Keep your heads up!' said the captain, Roy Keane,
  'Don't look so sad.'
Just before half-time, United got a corner,
David Beckham whipped in a cross so high, he said to
  himself, 'Lower, lower.'
The ball curled in the air and it hit someone's head,
It was the best goal Becks had ever seen
And who's head did it hit? The one and only Roy Keane.
Second half and United were controlling the game,
  Roy Keane was the rebel.
Then a throw-in was awarded to United, to be thrown by
  Gary Neville,
He threw it to Keane who made a great run,
He passed to Scholes, who passed to Cole - United's
  prodigal son.
He passed back to Keane who ran some more,
Suddenly 2-1 was the score.
The man who scored was one of the best players I've seen,
He's the captain of my favourite team and his name is . . .
Roy Keane!

Daniel Smith (13)
St Mary's CE High School, Downage

MY DREAM PARK

I wrote to the mayor of the town,
She looked at me with a frown
And turned my proposal down.

All I wanted was a park,
To go there when I wanted a little lark
And tease the dogs as they bark.

She said there was so little space,
You could not even drop a lace,
Let alone a park with a base.

I told her the town was boring
And the prices were always soaring,
And the canal's so small you can't get a boat mooring.

The mayor then said tough luck,
So I threatened to murder a duck,
But the guard threw me in some dog's muck.

In the night I covered her room in Sellotape
And I left a reminder of squashed grapes
Because I knew she would go rather ape.

When she came in, she did scream,
This is what happened, in her dream,
Then she tripped over a wooden beam.

She decided to give me the park I desired,
Then she had her entire staff fired,
Then for jobs, she had me hired.

The building plan went ahead,
I could see the park from my bed
And see the fences were made of lead.

Now I had what I was looking for,
As soon as it was open I was out the door,
Then I didn't want it any more.

Arjun Kumar Mittra (13)
St Mary's CE High School, Downage

APE ESCAPE

Anyone who's played Ape Escape will agree
That it's one of the best games of this century.
You gotta catch and evil monkey called Spector,
Who released some more chimps to help him take over the world.
If you haven't felt this experience, it's not too late,
You'll soon be playing this game that is so great,
If you're ready to part with your money,
You'll in no time be catching monkeys.
So put on your shoes and coat, then rush into town,
To your local games store, then go shop around.
Pick up a copy of Ape Escape from the store's new batch,
Quickly run to the counter with your wallet filled with cash.
When you get home put it in your PlayStation,
Then the 'start' screen appears, and then you can stop waiting.
You start to play and you feel really cool,
All other 'platform' games just have to drool,
But after a few minutes of play, you might lose heart
As there aren't any monkeys near the start.
But be patient, you'll have one in your sight,
That will start to panic and have a fright.
Then you chase it and it will start to fret
And then you know in a few seconds it'll be in your net!

Tyrone Hemmings (13)
St Mary's CE High School, Downage

THE HAG

There was once an old hag,
Who found life a drag,
And everything she did caused her to nag.

She owned a black cat
Which was very, very fat
And was born with the face of a bat.

They lived in an old house
Which was infested with lice
And stank with the stench of dead mice.

She didn't own a lot,
And was mentally starting to rot,
So she decided to change her ways . . . not!

She continued as before,
Still old and poor
And eventually died on her living-room floor.

Sim-Chung Tang (12)
St Mary's CE High School, Downage

SPARROW, SPARROW

Sparrow, sparrow up above,
Would you ever love a dove?

Would you ever swoop so low?
Could you ever sing that low?

Can you do loop the loop?
Would you like a Hula Hoop?

Do you fly with a crowd?
Are you as soft as a cloud?

Do you ever dance while you fly?
Could you ever tell a lie?

Do you have any friends?
Would you like to hear the end?

Motunrayo Onanuga (13)
St Mary's CE High School, Downage

FRIENDS

Friends are happy people,
Caring, sharing and true.
In school they are crazy
And some are a bit lazy,
But some are really cool,
And some just act like fools.
We eat a lot of candy,
And we have a friend called Mandy.
I have a friend, Christine,
She likes to be so pristine.
I have a friend called Imo,
And she owns a very big limo.
We also have a friend, Kimberley,
She wants to live in Wembley.
My friend, Christelle likes to talk a lot,
And she also likes to walk a lot.
All my friends are funny
When it's really sunny.
At the end of school
I like to go to the swimming pool.

Flossie Tecson (12)
St Mary's CE High School, Downage

THE SIGHT I SEE

When I stand up on the shore
I give myself a little tour
of all the wonders I can see
all around and in the sea.
The first thing that catches my eye
is the bright blue cloudless sky.
All the seagulls flying low
as the sea softly flows.
Then I hear a sudden splash
and that wonderful sight I see in a flash.
A dolphin and its young
swimming as they sung,
diving there in the sunset.
Then they start swimming fast, fast
like a jet and all of a sudden they disappeared.
Then I saw a man on the shore
just sitting there from night till dawn.
Then I came back the next day
and there that old man's body lay.
He had a lonely life
with no children or no wife.
Then I felt a teardrop on my face.
Then I walked home at a slow pace.

Holly Dooley (13)
St Mary's CE High School, Downage

AUTUMN

Drifting as the leaves fall down,
Leaves that are big, small, green or brown
Making crunching sounds on the ground.

Birds fly off to find a hotter place,
Others find spots to hibernate.

The place is cold, the place is damp,
The leaves on the floor shrivel, die and rot.

People freezing everywhere,
The trees have no leaves, they're stripped,
They're almost bare,
The place is cold outdoors and has wet floors.

Geu MacBullen (12)
St Mary's CE High School, Downage

FAIRY TALES, FAIRY TALE

F rogs, princesses and a prince
A dragon comes and hogs the castle
I n the castle are knights
R eady for a fight
Y ou will be amazed.

T he people are cheering
A ll the knights are singing
L ike they are fearing
E veryone is ready for the fight
S o are the knights.

F airies give the knights might
A lright knights you have to fight
I n they go to the dragon's cave
R oar goes the dragon
Y ou're in for a treat.

T he dragon says you're dead meat
A lright dragon you're going down to our feet
L ike you will give me a treat
E veryone had a seat.

Daniel Plaistow (12)
St Mary's CE High School, Downage

THE OLD OAK TREE

While the teachers sit in the buildings sipping their tea
no one knows what happens under the old oak tree.
There's Joe and Darren up to old tricks like
throwing conkers and fighting with sticks.
There's Jack and Daisy, Mike and Maisy trying
to break world records,
the longest kiss so far is an outstanding forty-two seconds.
There's Joseph and Luke the brainy group,
discussing traffic and easy routes.
There's Bill and Bob the lazy mob,
they slouch and growl, they're known as slobs.
Then there's the crazy posse, John, Joe and Jack
doing impressions of poor old Mr Black.

Imogen Katz (12)
St Mary's CE High School, Downage

CHRISTMAS

Christmas is an annual festival on December 25th.
We commemorate the birth of Christ on this day.
The days leading up to Christmas are hectic,
Shops are packed and food is being bought everywhere.
Do you remember when you were young and you asked
Father Christmas for presents in the shopping malls
And he never gave you what you wanted?
Why is that?
But whatever the reason, I'm sure it's a good one.
Anyway, enjoy Christmas because it only comes once a year
And the end of the world may be near.
You've been warned.

Marvin Davidson (12)
St Mary's CE High School, Downage

MY CAT

I have a cat who can be fun one minute,
Then run away the next.
I wish I had a rabbit or a dog,
Maybe a mouse or a pig.
I would love to have something other than a cat.

Oh how I wish I could have something like a hamster,
Maybe one I could go camping with, or a poodle.
I had a dream once that I had a really cute, cuddly, pink rat.
I don't know why I dreamed that.

But when I'm alone in my room,
My lovely, lazy, fluffy, tabby cat comes to cheer me up.
He loves to sleep and never plays with string,
Or even a ball.
My mum always says he likes me,
But I don't always think he does.

My nan has a lovely, black, furry cat
Whose eyes are as green as green.
He always plays with everything I put in his path,
He even picks up foil and brings it back to everyone,
Then he loves to chase lots of string.

My nan's cat's called Wax,
My tabby cat's called Tom,
But then again he always cheers me up,
               although he's lazy,
But most of all, he's my lovely, lazy, fluffy, tabby cat.

Clare Lenton (12)
St Mary's CE High School, Downage

WHY PICK ON ME?

I didn't do anything wrong today
And hardly said a word,
Yet they still decided to pick on me,
It's starting to get absurd.

I was getting my books from my locker
And starting to go down the hall,
When I saw my worst enemies ever,
Usually five, but seven in all.

I started to run for my classroom,
But a sly foot came under my shoes,
I nearly went flying towards them,
Instead I ran, with nothing to lose.

I heard a pounding of footsteps
As the bullies came running behind,
Then I ran into the car park,
Looking for somewhere to hide.

They weren't as dumb as I suspected
And each grabbed one of my limbs,
I thought the world was over
until Xenia stepped in.

She told them to leave me alone
And that I'd had enough,
She took one bold step before me
Then they told her she wasn't so tough.

They grabbed at her neatly tied hair
And spat in her young, pretty face,
She was wrestled on to the floor
And hit repeatedly in the face.

They didn't forget much about me
And threw me onto the floor,
They made my head crack open,
Then chucked me into the bin. What for?

Xenia then followed behind me
And broke her nose on the way,
I then fell unconscious,
In the dust and dirt we lay.

I woke in a nearby hospital
With a sore and throbbing head,
I couldn't remember what had happened
And just wanted to stay in bed.

A week and a half later,
Xenia and I moved school,
The bullies were soon expelled
Which we both found really cool!

If ever you are to be bullied,
Never give in at all,
Tell a trusted teacher
And you'll be respected in school.

Laura Payne (12)
St Mary's CE High School, Downage

LUNCH

Today is the famous spaghetti day,
The greatest day of the week,
But little miss 'I'm on a diet'
Always chooses leek.

For pudding it's the usual,
Apple and crumble and pie,
With lumpy, bumpy custard
That makes you wanna die. Aargh!

Monday it's pie and chips,
Tuesday it's bangers and mash,
Wednesday it's pasta,
Mr Lettuce pays in cash.

Thursday it's chicken,
Friday it's spaghetti,
At the end of the week
You'll have a *big* belly.

Bianca Fough (12)
St Mary's CE High School, Downage

MILLENNIUM

The millennium is so near,
Yet so far.
Some people are excited,
But some people don't care.
There'll be big parties,
There'll be small parties.
Everyone will be having fun,
But most of all
It's going to be big.

Chris Skordis (14)
St Mary's CE High School, Downage

I'M EATING

I eat an apple everyday,
My mother says, 'It keeps the doctors away.'
My brother says, it hurts his jaws.
My sister cries, 'I can't eat anymore.'
My baby brother loves to eat,
Especially raw meat,
Daddy smiles when he eats the toast,
At Christmas he makes the roast,
Bill my mate and his girl Jill Tate,
Eat salads and loads of pickles,
His sister Kim loves to be tickled,
My cousin Jack says nothing at all,
His dad runs a stall,
In school I play with my friends,
Run around until the end,
The birds fly in the sky,
What do they eat? Apples too?
No silly, bird stew.

Rubina Pausker (12)
St Mary's CE High School, Downage

STARS

Stars are bright, they shine all night,
Like people watching over us,
They're our guardian angels, helping
Us in every possible way they can.
They're like jewels in a satin, gold case,
Some are like dolphins swimming in space,
Like God's doing miracles for the poor and hungry,
Stars are wondrous and beautiful
And will enlighten you, stars.

Jason Fester (14)
St Mary's CE High School, Downage

Millennium

Parties in the streets,
The year 2000 is almost here,
Blinding lights,
This is the best time of year.

People visiting churches,
Food on the tables,
Holy people praying,
Priests telling fables.

Shopping precincts are very busy,
Not a sad face anywhere,
Cash machines are being used,
People spend and spend like they don't care.

The next day I am tired,
The parties have ceased,
New babies being born,
The bankruptcy level has increased.

My computer isn't working,
The Millennium Bug has passed,
All the money put to a waste,
The new year went too fast.

Michael Fowler (12)
St Mary's CE High School, Downage

Blue

Blue is the colour of the endless sky,
It has that special feeling that makes you feel high.

It moves through our minds like the rapid waves of the sea,
You feel as relaxed as the sea could ever be.

Blue is noble, just like the Queen,
In our hearts it has to be seen.

Blue reigns the sky, when the sun is gone,
There sleeps the world, until the day is born.

Subathra Sivanandan (11)
St Mary's CE High School, Downage

WEATHER

When the weather is hot you always want to sunbathe,
When the weather is cold it is as cold as a cave,
When the weather wants to snow you want to make a snowman,
When the weather wants to hail you run for safety as soon as you can,
When the weather is sunny you always go out to play,
When the weather is cloudy you wonder if you should go out to play.
All the time the weather changes his mind how he would like to be,
He may use his wind to make a whirlpool in the sea,
He may use snow to cover up the roads.
With his weather we can do things like sunbathe and play all on
                                                                   a sunny day,
We can freeze and be cold but never get told if the weather is going
                                                                    to be the same.
The weather always changes his mind as to what he wants to be as
                                                                    you can see,
If he has a toothache he makes a hurricane,
If he has a cough he makes a bang of thunder.
If he has a blow torch he makes a flash of lightning.
My goodness gracious I don't believe the weather cannot stay the same.

Carla Powell (12)
St Mary's CE High School, Downage

A Rotten Tooth

There was once a girl
Who had a rotten tooth.
It had a really bad root,
She ate lots of cake,
That's why she had *toothache!*

She went to the dentist
To pull it out,
But just about . . . then,
She had to scream
Because her tummy wanted *ice-cream!*

She ran out of the dentist chair
For her tummy could not bear
Another minute without
That delicious creamy taste
Of the soft vanilla paste.

She ran to the ice-cream van
Whose owner's name was Dan,
And asked for ice-cream 99.

As she licked and licked her ice-cream
And strolled her way home,
She met her mother full of steam,
Raring to go . . .
Back to the dentist . . . *pronto!*

When she sat back in the chair
And noticed a pair of pliers!
She opened her mouth to scream for help,
Then the dentist said,
'Oh, I've pulled the wrong tooth out!'

Jade Georgiou (12)
St Mary's CE High School, Downage

A Vet's Nightmare

A crocodile cried
With a terrible pain,
He had toothache
Driving him insane.

He went to the vet
Who said, 'Open Wide.'
The man looked in
And down his throat he did glide.

Another vet came,
'Your teeth are too bad,
They'll all have to come out!'
Now that's very sad.

A third vet came along
With great big pliers.
'I'll pull your teeth out,
I'll use this wire.'

He was too cruel
So I bit off his hand,
He sailed into orbit,
Came back, bruised but tanned.

'Don't be a wimp,
Don't be a sook.'
A fourth vet was there
So he took a look.

He took my tooth out
With no fuss at all,
So now I still
Can be cool.

Hannah Compton (12)
St Mary's CE High School, Downage

ROCKY THE RHINO

I'm Rocky the rhino,
You'd better not mess with me.
I'm as swift as a cheetah,
I sting like a bee.
So remember don't mess with me.

I'm Rocky the rhino,
I'm as big as two boulders,
I have no worries on my shoulders
Because I run things round here.

I'm Rocky the rhino,
I'm as grey as my owner's lino.
If you mess with me you'll be off in a hurry
Because I'm . . . Rocky the rhino.

Rochelle Davids (13)
St Mary's CE High School, Downage

MAN UNITED

The crowd went mad when Shezza scored,
There was no moment I was bored.
I watched Man U play as they should
I've never seen them play so good.
Becks got hurt, he carried on,
He has a scar, the pain has gone.
The second goal was in the air,
It came from Scholes, and caused despair.
No doubt about it, the brightest star,
United are the best by far!
We snatched the double, held it tight,
Fergie's army proved their might.

Jasmine Ahmed (13)
St Mary's CE High School, Downage

THE TALE OF THE OLD ONES

The world was young, the mountains green,
No stain yet on the moon was seen.
No letters were on tree or stone,
The woods were standing all alone.
No foot yet on the paths had been tread,
When life from the north had quickly fled.
The peaks of the north were out of sight,
When gates of stars had opened wide.

The old ones came in mighty ships,
That sailed the air, but not the seas.
They made the stars, which shine so bright,
They filled the sun with awesome light.
They made the humans, elves and dwarfs
And also made the treacherous orcs.
But gates of stars would shine no more,
Their ships were levelled with the floor.

A darkness spread all through the land,
The moon was grey, the seas were dead.
This news the elves could never bear,
Their star had faded in despair.
The halls of dwarfs forever shut,
The orcs were dead and nothing but . . .
But out of darkness came a light,
The human race has still survived.

Valery Katerinchuk (12)
St Mary's CE High School, Downage

DYING

The birds are singing,
They sing no more.
The dogs are barking,
They bark no more.
The gangs are coming,
I must now hide.
They shoot!
They kill!
They terrorise!
People crying
But they are laughing.
Laughing! What is laughing?
Having a smile on your face,
Face, face, what is a face?
A place that is safe.
Safe, safe, what is safe?
You are not safe in a dying place.
Dying, lying, cold as ice,
You are as still as a grain of rice.

Raphael V Griffith (12)
St Mary's CE High School, Downage

MY LOVE

Ever since that night
I liked you from the start
You were never off my mind
Your love I want to find.

I want to be with you
And for us to never part
To show how much I care
And how much I want to share.

To me you're really special
So gentle and so kind
I want us to be together
And cherish every time.

All I want to say
Is keep a space in your heart
For the one and only me
'Cause *I love you.*

Velma Candy (13)
St Mary's CE High School, Downage

CRICKET

C owardly walked onto the pitch.
R ain came before they could start the match.
I ntelligent people decided not to play.
C racked his bat against the wall.
K icked the ball and hurt his foot.
E ntered the room in joy.
T ry to run away from the game.

B atted the ball when he was called onto the pitch.
A cted sick because he wasn't called Rick.
T humped his head and thought he was dead.

A ngrily got up and started to shout.
N ervously walked onto the pitch.
D ropped the ball when he could have caught it.

B atted the ball
A ll the way to the boundary line.
L ost the match, but went home in joy.
L oves cricket very much and wants to be in the team next year.

Kunal Jadeja (12)
St Mary's CE High School, Downage

THE FURRY CATERPILLAR

I am a furry caterpillar,
I live in the forest,
It's hot, wet and damp here,
Especially in this tree.
I am very colourful,
My skin is red and orange
And if someone tries to eat me
I roll into a ball and pretend
I'm the fire,
To please my desire.
The leaves down here are very green,
But as they fall, they rot
And roll and die upon the soil,
The rain is usually dripping,
It always tips and taps,
I sometimes think I'm sinking,
Sinking down and down,
Overall I'm happy now,
Happy as can be,
So I'll see you later,
'Bye-bye everybody.'

Christine Neumann (12)
St Mary's CE High School, Downage

THE WAY OF WEATHER

The weather can be rainy,
The weather can be sunny.
There are good things about weather,
There are bad things about weather.

Nobody can trust the weather,
It can be terrifying and scary,
It can be hot and sunny
Or it can be worse.

The weather can destroy places,
The weather can be peaceful.
It can be both,
So we cannot trust the weather.

Kamran Golami (12)
St Mary's CE High School, Downage

TEACHERS

Some teachers are good,
Some teachers are bad,
Some teachers are funny,
Some teachers are mad.

Some teachers are hairy,
Some teachers are bald,
Some teachers are kind
But don't be fooled.

Some teachers scream
And other teachers whine,
Some teachers are ugly
And others are fine.

Some teachers smell nice,
Some teachers reek,
Some teachers yell
And others speak.

So in the end
We really can't tell,
Whether teachers are from heaven,
Or whether they're from hell.

Kieren Russell (13)
St Mary's CE High School, Downage

FRANK THE FOOL

Frank the fool, late for work as usual,
Racing down the stairs in a hurry, slipped and fell in last night's curry,
Grabbed his coat and grabbed his hat, accidentally kicked the cat,
Walking fast down the busy street, tripping on his two left feet,
Frank sees his bus and makes a dash, only to find he's forgotten
                                                                              his cash,
Frank decides to walk all the way, little did he know this would be
                                                                              his final day,
Frank saw the bus, big and red, little did he know he would soon
                                                                              be dead,
Frank was hit and fell to the ground, concerned people crowded around,
Frank was dead, skid marks across his head,
Up to heaven Frank did go, to meet his wife, whose name was Joe.

Michael Mazur (13)
St Mary's CE High School, Downage

ICE HOCKEY

I like ice hockey,
It's fast and rough,
To play it you have to be tough.
You get chucked into the wall,
You take a little stumble and then you fall,
You play the game with a puck,
To win you can't rely on luck,
You have to play the game
With a lot of skill,
It's not over till
The horn goes!

Philip Brian Powis-Vasey (12)
St Mary's CE High School, Downage

CYCLING DOWN THE STREET POEM

I jump on my bike
and ride down the street.
Turn round the bend,
Whiz past the library
heading for my friend's house.

The road bends sharply at Puijold Lane
like a broken arm.
I brush past the shrubs
alongside the pavement
and pass Batty's farm.

Tired gasp and strain and bend
climbing Hallow's Slope.
Then flying down the other side
just like an antelope.

Swanking into Johnie's street,
Cycling hands on hips,
Past O'Connors' cornershop
that always smells of chips.

Bump the door of his garage
where we always have some fun,
Lean my bike
and knock at the door,
'Can John come out to play?'

Louis Mateega (13)
St Mary's CE High School, Downage

COWBOYS IN A TOWN

A cowboy holding a silver pistol walked in the city,
Came to a bar and ordered a glass of beer.
Another cowboy came to the city to have a fight with him,
Everybody was quiet and looking at them.
Both of them are ready to fight,
They went outside and took their pistols out, ready to fight.
Everyone was far away from them,
Ashes, dust, car, noise was among them,
But they don't care. They only care about the fight.
They took a long step and when the red lamp is on they have to shoot.
One and two and three, the red lamp is on.
Every car stopped moving.
Bang, bang, bang, bang!
Both of them are just shooting at each other.
The cowboy with a silver pistol walked to the other cowboy,
The other cowboy was lying on the floor.
Everyone was silent.
The winner was the cowboy with the silver pistol.
The cowboy who was lying on the floor was taken away by ambulance.
Police arrested the cowboy with the silver pistol.
The game is over!

Oki Sampurno (14)
St Mary's CE High School, Downage

SWIMMING

I love swimming, it's really fun,
It keeps you healthy, but doesn't help you run.
Splashing in the water,
Swallowed in the swirls.
Trying to jump the waves
Is the best thing in the world.

Jumping off the diving board
Is another exciting thing.
Spinning in the air,
Breeze whizzing through your hair.
Suddenly you're in the water
And everything comes to an end!

Amma Ansomaa Brefo (12)
St Mary's CE High School, Downage

WHAT IS LIFE?

They say that life is a world of pleasure and happiness,
Just waiting to be set upon,
Comfort and love are yours too,
That's how they define life.

But for me things are very different,
Hatred and disaster are my words for life,
I wish I was dead,
Then I wouldn't have to go through with all this pain.

My parents always used to fight,
Hitting me and each other.
I used to get beat-up at school,
But nobody cared.

I never had any friends,
Just evil thoughts in my head.
Been in jail three times,
Orphaned by my parents at the age of ten.

But still I have to go on,
Carrying out sins to survive.
Is this how life should be?
Because if it is, I don't want to be a part of it.

Rajiv Varsani (13)
St Mary's CE High School, Downage

THE GOAT

There was a man, now please take note,
There was a man, who had a goat,
He loved that goat, indeed he did,
He loved that goat, just like a kid.

One day, that goat felt frisky and fine,
Ate three red shirts from off the line.
The man who grabbed him by the back,
Tied him to a railroad track.

But when the train drove into sight,
That goat grew pale and green with fright.
He heaved a sigh, as if in pain,
Coughed up those shirts and flagged the train.

Valerie Usuanlele-Beckley (11)
St Mary's CE High School, Downage

THE WINDOW

The world through a window has bad deeds,
With horrible weather and bad beings,
The trees and leaves,
Grass and seeds
Are brown, crispy and dry
But in the outside,
Standing by nature,
Has wonderful skies and seas,
The glaciers, the flowers
Are all beautiful to me.

James Osborn (11)
St Mary's CE High School, Downage

I LIKE PINK

Pink is the colour of a pig,
It's a marvellous colour,
Nice and pink,
Kind and generous pink.
It is my favourite colour,
So I guess it's a favourite colour,
A pink cot and a pink chair,
Could it possibly be mine?
Oh, it's not just mine.
Loving pink,
Oh, so simple,
You love it as well as me,
Red and white make pink.

Gemma Williams (11)
St Mary's CE High School, Downage

THE DREADED DEMON

D readed fear fills people's hearts when they hear its piercing scream.
E veryone who looks into its fearsome eyes are turned into marble instantly.
M onstrous eyes like flames of fire dancing, melting its victims' happiness.
O range corn snakes are its long locks of hair. Its lips are like silver nail polish glistening in the light.
N ever has anyone come out of the Black Forest alive.

Nicola Stephenson (11)
St Mary's CE High School, Downage

MY HOLIDAY

I arrive at the beach,
Finally I am here,
The world is my oyster,
I hear the ocean,
Wind blowing through my hair,
The earth moves,
I feel free!
It's paradise,
The beach glowing,
The sun beaming,
The sky blue,
The clouds are like little balls of wool,
The waves crashing against the pier,
Heaven is here,
The surfers catching a massive wave,
Seagulls calling,
Suddenly the dream ends.

Scott Shelley (13)
St Mary's CE High School, Downage

TRANSPARENCY

If everything was glass
I could read your thoughts
And I could see your dreams,
Now everything is fake it seems,
Nothing is real anymore,
It's all army tanks and war,
Nobody stops to think any more
About plants and animals,
Lying, dying on the floor,
Nobody cares anymore.

Mark Davie (12)
St Mary's CE High School, Downage

GOD AND HIS HEAVEN

There is a place up above,
Full of wonder,
Full of love,
Up there is good, not bad
And no one is ever sad,
This place has a wonderful name,
It's a lot more precious than a hall of fame,
It's called heaven.

Everyone is having fun,
Children are running around in the shady sun,
All is peaceful, all is calm,
Their world is full of wonder and grace,
This world is heaven also in His palm,
No one is an outcast in His world,
They all have a place.

God Almighty,
The great I am,
Gave us His son,
The holy lamb,
Your Earthly friends may fail you
And change with changing years,
These friends are always worthy
Of those dear names they bear.

Leon Gordon-Ailey (11)
St Mary's CE High School, Downage

MY TEDDY BEAR

When I was small I had the most fantastic teddy bear,
It came with me almost everywhere,
In my bed, in the bath, at dinner, at lunch, in the playground
where it stopped to have fun!
But one day I lost it and I can't find it,
Is it here, is it there, is it anywhere?
'Mum have you seen my bear?'
'No honey, look over there.'
After looking for it, I went upstairs and there was my
teddy bear on my bed.

Priya Makwana (13)
St Mary's CE High School, Downage

I WILL PUT IN MY BOX

Some glittering stars on a dark blue night,
A gleaming moon shining on God's green Earth,
A burning sun glowing on the busy towns.

      I will put in my box

An ice-cube that never melts,
Water that never freezes,
A flying bird under the sea.

> I will put in my box

My box is fashioned with silver lining and golden pearls
With moons on the lid and mysteries in the corners
And its hinges are made of dinosaur bones.

> I will put in my box

I shall surf in my box
On the jungle floor
And surf up into the busy city.

Jeremy Boamah (11)
St Mary's CE High School, Downage

THE STRANGER

He wandered alone down the bustling streets,
his tired head hanging, his weary arms drooped.
His clothes were tattered, ripped and damp
and all he did was walk.

His face was battered, torn and scarred,
his eyes so dull, so weary, so lost.
He hung his head desolately and dragged his weary feet,
as he walked slowly on.

He stumbled and staggered, lost and alone,
his spirit broken and dead.
He had nowhere to go and no one to see,
so all he did was walk.

Annabel Grossman (13)
South Hampstead High School

THE STRUGGLE FOR LIFE

Embedded in the scorching hot sand,
I lay there silently.
Peter and Darkie asleep,
Whilst I pray.

The burning rays of sun,
From the previous day,
Dawns on me that this is no dream.
Being in the vast areas
Of the Australian desert,
Relying on an uncivilised
Black Aboriginal boy
Makes me feel inadequate
And not like a big sister.

Fears, that the boy's
Abandoning me amongst
The blanket of desert,
Dappled by sunlight,
Arises and worries me.
Peter forgetting his old life,
With Mama, Papa . . . and me.

I dread tomorrow,
Another day of trekking,
Small rations of food
And the ludicrous behaviour
Of Peter.

I aspire, to reach Adelaide
And from this dream,
To jump back into reality
To face another hard struggle,
Of staying alive.

Selina Tang (11)
South Hampstead High School

The Desert

I sit here alone,
watching the sun set throw amber lights about.
Another day is gone,
another day without civilisation.
Will we ever get back?

The boys play in the river,
I am calling Peter,
he ignores me,
he does not respect me anymore.
Will they leave me here alone?

Peter is so friendly with the 'darkie',
I feel he might be mislead,
no longer do I hear his cry for help,
no longer does he hold my hand for comfort.
Will he forget civilisation?

I feel thirsty,
but I dare not drink from the water with that naked boy
I feel hungry,
but I cannot bring myself to ask him for food.
Will I die like this?

I hear the distant howl of a distraught dingo,
the rustle of impatient branches on a tree,
the crimson specks of fireflies buzz busily about
I remember the jumping ants.
Can he protect us?

He is clean and tidy,
like civilisation,
but he is black and naked,
so he cannot be.
What will happen to me?

Venetia Rainey (11)
South Hampstead High School

MARY'S POEM

Waiting for the flames to come sinking into sand
White heat horror, numbness
Now in the cool of the night we are alone,
I hold his hand and the fear ebbs away.

A visitor, a wombat curiously smells us
A female tigercat sizes us up, but leaves
Under a rainbow sky: amber, crimson, scarlet, jade and emerald
We awake.

The blazing sun shines down upon us
As we begin a long journey through a strange world
Thirst and hunger, I'm dizzy but he needs me.

After days we see food, great bunches of juicy fruit
We feast. New tastes, new feelings
Hope spreads inside me
I see how beautiful this land of wonder is.

A kookaburra squawks merrily above
Startled it's gone. The shrill voice of my brother.
I run to find a naked black boy, staring
I look away, embarrassed.

My brother likes him. Our journey begins.

Natalie Simpson-Hassell (11)
South Hampstead High School

I Lay Here

I lay here, deeply buried in sand.
Lying, watching the sky.
The quiet desolate moon shines a clear light on the whole carpet of the Australian desert.

I listen, closely, to the soft rattling of my brother's breath,
To the quiet sound of leaves rustling and to a kookaburra's shrilling cry somewhere off in the distance. At daytime the desert is awake and full of life, but yet now, at night, it is calm, quite cold and sedated.

I fear, that the boys will leave me to kindle my own fire, to hunt my own food. And I fear most that I might never see another home again besides the desert.

I wonder, if we'll run out of food or if Peter will forget his old life or he'll forget me, his sister.

I wish, Peter would look up to me more, I wish I was younger so I could join in the fun between the two boys instead of having to stand aside and watch disapprovingly.

I know, tomorrow will come, the kookaburra will call,
and when day breaks it will be the continuation of a long struggle to stay alive.

Rebecca Perlman (11)
South Hampstead High School

LOST

Thoughts flower through the maze of mind,
Cold, harsh dread through my shaken body,
Picture of my parents, my home, my friends on the horizon so far,
Waiting, longingly under the gang-gang trees.

When can we go home?
When will we be rescued?
I don't know, can I survive another day, another night in
this arid desert?
Waiting, longingly under the gang-gang trees.

The horizon flickers shades of orange, scarlet and lilac silhouetted
against the ever patient sky,
Curious of the bush boy's movements,
Silly to trust him, but the alternative . . . 'death'
Deep down I do trust him.
Is Peter being led astray?
Am I not wanting any longer?
I wallow in self pity,
Waiting longingly under the gang-gang trees.

What's behind that tree over there?
What's around that bend over there?
Where is that path leading?
Where are the answers?
What hidden dangers lie waiting for me?
Waiting, longingly under the gang-gang trees.

The black boy is naked,
So embarrassing and so offensive,
I suppose I will have to put up with it,
After all he is my food and water,
Yet Peter does not see me as his life force,
Waiting, longingly under the gang-gang trees.

My parents (my world), where are you in my hour of need?
Peter and I yearn for civilisation, as we knew it,
How long will we last?
There has to be a way out of this desperation,
Waiting, longingly under the gang-gang trees.

Saba Yussouf (11)
South Hampstead High School

OUT IN THE DESERT

In desert silence Mary stood,
What would they do for water and food?
Terrified of being alone,
How would they ever get back home?

As the sun came up the animals awoke,
The kookaburra sang with a dreadful croak.
The ants attacked with an awful bite,
What animals would scare them in the night?

The brigallow had a strong scented smell,
The eucalyptus gave shade as well.
Quandong fruit was good to eat,
Ground vines coiled and clutched at their feet.

They found a bush boy ebony black,
Was he the one who could get them back?
At home a black boy was someone to hate,
Out in the desert he would be a good mate.

Elizabeth Elster (11)
South Hampstead High School

OFF TO SCHOOL AGAIN

Each night when my head hits the pillow,
I fall sound asleep, snoring quietly.
The dribble trickles down my chin,
A smile forms on my face.

I smell the smoke, billowing over everyone,
There are rising flames, golden, amber.
The school lies like glowing coals,
But everyone gets out alive.

The sirens wail, teachers panic,
I am sweating in the heat.
There is no one in the building,
My mind is at rest.

I wake up, to find that school beckons,
Breakfast is munched, clothes pulled on.
I set off, plodding down the street,
Bag slung nonchalantly over shoulder.

The lessons proceed, the day passes in a haze,
Homework is set, and I meander home again.
Dinner is eaten, and pyjamas are on.
I flop into bed, exhausted.

I hear the screams for help, a trickle through the ceiling.
Then powdered plaster crashes to the floor.
A heaving wave surges through the school.
Murky green surrounds me.

Children are drowning, swim to the door.
I let the water roll over me, carrying me to the exit.
My maths teacher is gasping for breath,
Pulled under by the strong current.

The curtains are drawn, sunlight floods in.
I sit up, and greet my mother grumpily.
A glass of milk, button my shirt,
Off to school again.

Rebecca Herman (12)
South Hampstead High School

MARY'S POEM

It was boiling
When I awoke.
I was scared.
Were we ever
Going to get home?
Were we going
To find help?
There were little
Cockatoos flying around,
With a tiger-cat
Pouncing up and down.
The red hot sand was
Burning my feet
As I walked around,
And the fresh sound
Of water rushing excitedly.
We were alone,
Frightened,
I heard birds humming
A sweet song,
So I sat down by
Peter and listened.

Stephanie Horn (11)
South Hampstead High School

EARLY MORNING CRIES

As the dusk parts and the dawn makes its way,
into the beginning of another day.
The sound of the morning fill the air,
as the world awakes without a care.
I watch the birds soaring round in the sky,
I look at the plants growing up high.
I hear the animals walking around
and there's Peter, not making a sound.
The Aboriginal boy is by his side,
I can see he has a secret that he's trying to hide.
The Mopoke waddles into sight,
The dingo after him gives me a fright.
I can see new colours including jade,
Reseda and amber hide in the shade.
The crimson gives beauty to the sunrise,
all these things bring tears to my eyes.
I must not worry for Peter's sake,
because there are two lives that are at stake.
Peter grumbles then rubs his eye,
he gives a big yawn for such a small guy.
He goes over to the Aborigine and gives him a tap,
I feel like I've lost him like there's now a gap.
The aborigine stands up and beckons to go,
Oh Mummy and Daddy, I miss you so.

Lauren Cooney (11)
South Hampstead High School

SCHOOLDAYS

In the corner,
Waiting, anxious,
Crouched in the shadows,
Tiresome, longing,
The bells ring,
The bullies are coming.

Your inner body,
Tight, revolving,
Your face against wall,
Lifeless, broken,
Haunting footsteps,
You pretend you're asleep,
The bullies are here,
You are suddenly woken.

Sliding down on the floor,
Tiresome, lifeless,
The door handle moves,
Creaking, bewitched,
The door pulls clear,
The bullies have pitched.

Footsteps, closer,
Depressed, tired,
Hitting punching,
Your shrieks drown away,
You remember,
They'll be there same time, next day.

Elizabeth Rawlings (12)
South Hampstead High School

DID TIM WATERS EVER GET CAUGHT?

It was a cloudy Monday morning
I really didn't want to go!
I could feel a frosty breeze through the rough window
Just as the trouble began to flow.

I sat right in the centre of the daunting classroom
I sit in front of *Tim*,
It's never really fair because
I have always detested him.

'Jane do this to her, John do that!'
Tim shrieked in the background,
I couldn't bear the piercing noise they made.
Why do I have to be so fat?

It's not my fault.
Why do they do it to me?
I don't understand,
They don't even care, as far as I can see.

Whilst I can hear them whispering
I just try to ignore them
By sitting as still as a frightened rabbit,
As my heart starts thundering.

I wish the teacher would catch them.
'Then they'll be done' I thought to myself.
This time I knew I had been saved
When the teacher walked in.

'Whatever is going on in here?' She boomed at us.
A smile crept up my cheeks towards my ears.
Tim was caught, once and for all.
Now what's he going to say about that?

But no, I was wrong and distraught
Tim Waters never did get caught!

Danielle Gertner (12)
South Hampstead High School

SKOOLDAYS

i feel asleap in Latin,
spraned my ankel in PE
i wos showted at in maths
becos i coodn't count to 3.

inglish was a problem,
i dident have my book.
the storey i had rote
teecher dident look.

i blu up the lab in siense
that dident go down well.
i think i'll say my day at skool
wos even worse than hel!

Alice Edgerley (12)
South Hampstead High School

BUDDIES

Choose your buddy for the trip,
The words are like sharp knives,
He knows nobody wants him,
So he stays in his chair,
His heart is pounding.

His eyes begin to water,
His head begins to ache,
He blinks back the tears,
Snaps his eyes into focus
And puts on a brave face.

Just because he's different,
Just because he's black,
It doesn't mean he's nasty,
He's actually kinder than most,
But no one would notice that.

A small boy approaches him
And timidly whispers a question,
They both smile warm smiles
And from then on they are buddies,
Not just for the field trip but for life.

Isobel Freeman (12)
South Hampstead High School

A Fatal Warning

A shadow passes the alley where I hide
A shadow that fills me with dread
A shadow that has the potential to kill
A shadow that clouds the road ahead.

A shadow in the guise of a feline
A shadow that clutches my heart
A shadow that devours all of my kind
And piles then up on death's own cart.

My little grey kind live in a constant fear
Of who he will take on the morrow.
My little grey kind live in a constant fear
And all hang their heads in their sorrow.

By day, we creep to avoid him,
By night we weep in our beds,
He has a knack of knowing just where we are
No one is spared, they all end up *dead*

No one can predict who will be the next victim,
Will it be mouse or bird, vole or rat?
But whoever you are, be you vole, bird or mouse,
I tell you, implore you, *beware of the cat!*

Laura Vignoles (12)
South Hampstead High School

FRIENDSHIP

A friend is someone who you can always trust,
You tell secret by secret laughing away,
Loyal and caring this person must,
With a smile that welcomes you every day.

Not just a friend must this person be to you,
With the kind and caring welcoming heart,
But a friend to her you must be too,
For with friendship there is not just one part.

Not always is there happiness,
An argument sometimes takes place,
But your friendship is not any less
And it always ends up with a smile on your face.

As you lay awake at night looking forward to tomorrow,
You think of the many cheeky things you get up to,
She will always be there when you are in any sorrow,
To brighten up your day as you would do too.

Tatiana Los (13)
South Hampstead High School

FRIENDS

Friends are always there for you,
Willing to care and share,
They are people who you can trust and be honest towards,
Without friends life would be dull.

Friends have got many good and bad qualities,
They can make you laugh when you are feeling down,
They are always there in times of need and trouble,
Friends brighten up your life.

Friends are not always all that charming,
All friends have their arguments and bad patches,
In times of hate and selfishness,
True friendship is all about trust and loyalty.

At school you can play together and share happy times,
On the weekends you can meet up together and have a laugh,
Friends are always generous and kind-hearted,
Friends are important to all people and without them we
Would all be alone.

Sabrina Paramesh (12)
South Hampstead High School

FRIENDSHIP

Friendship, what does it mean?
Such a nice feeling,
Sharing,
Those secret thoughts meant for just the two of us
Remembering,
Those special experiences, on school trips,
Nights spent chattering and giggling till midnight
Trusting,
Each other forever
Growing,
Changing becoming an individual, yet together
Spending,
Long summer evenings, hiding in the woods,
Just the two of us, hoping they would never end.
Friendship - knowing that the bond will never be broken.

Leora Graham (12)
South Hampstead High School

FRIENDSHIP

Friendship is the meaning of many things.
It's the foundation of any relationship.
Friendship is known for the happiness it brings,
It brings out the ease in a hardship.

Some say friendship is a windy road that holds many ups and downs.
Many seem to think that friendship is a gift from the heavens above.
People often picture friendship to be the smile that replaces a frown.
Others would often gesture friendship to be a factor of love.

A friend is someone who will catch you when you fall.
A pal is someone who you count on to always be there when you're sad.
The friend's priority to you is set higher than a castle wall.
The pal has the ability to make it better even if it is that bad.

Friendship can be held between two colleagues who share a chuckle every day.
It can be experienced by lovers who dream about each other at night.
Friendship can be unknowingly tied between toddlers who always fight and rarely play.
It can be inherited between families who can make the members' day bright.

So have you experienced a friendship that you feel is really special?
Many people have friends that they really can relate to.
But are you really a friend that others would be lucky to have?
Truthful people take a long time to answer this, what about you?

Stefanie Stavri (12)
South Hampstead High School

LONDON

As you enter the dirty streets of busy London
the pollution immediately hits you,
The nasty, disgusting smell just waits for you to breathe in
the horrid smoke and pollute your body,
The indecent fumes roar out of big cars vigorously,
along with harmful oil as well,
No wonder there is such a big worry over global warming.

'Can I have some change,' you often hear from old savages,
who waste all their money on alcohol,
'Please, I have no home,' another would cry wearing rags
that they could just about afford,
You would see all of these people along the street
asking for their pittance,
Imagine if all your money came from people's odd
generosity among the streets.

'Ey, you move it up,' would be the various cries of drivers
with road rage,
All the hectic racket of constant beeps, or rude comments
coming out of noisy, roaring cars,
The blaring radios turned up loud enough to deafen the
person inside the cars,
Topless male posers showing off with all windows down,
in their Porsches or whatever small cars and their roaring engines
really make the rush hour something to look forward to.

Kate Evangeli (11)
South Hampstead High School

READY FOR ANYTHING

I sat in the class,
Searching for the face,
The face which glares,
The face which never turns away,
I was going to get him today,
I was going to scream, kick and fight I was,
I was ready for him,
I was ready for anything,
The door creaked open,
Loud, thumping footsteps came towards me,
He was hideous,
His face scrunched up,
Eyes wide open, mouth slightly apart,
A big muscular arm flew straight at my face,
The throbbing pain sprung out of me,
I thought I was ready,
Ready for anything,
But I wasn't and now I know.

Lina Harfouche (12)
South Hampstead High School

FRIENDSHIP

Friendship is a very important thing in life,
A real friend is someone that cares for you but not spites you,
A real friend is someone that you can tell all your secrets to,
and to know she won't tell anyone,
A real friend is someone you can trust, someone that is loyal
and that will always be there for you.
Someone who is fun to be with and to spend your weekends with,
This is a real friend.

To be a real friend is another story,
You need to be kind and caring,
Fun and noisy
But at times a shoulder to lean on,
And of course there's the keeping secrets factor . . .
Can you figure out the rest?

Yasemin Dil (12)
South Hampstead High School

THE LOSS OF A FRIEND

The words hit me hard and fast, like a bullet from a gun
Normally the tears come first, but for me, I had nothing.

I looked towards the faces around, begging it not to be true
But from the sights passed back, gave me the impossible truth
I already knew.

For days I lay around just thinking, common sense was what I lacked,
I truly thought wishing 'ifs' and 'buts' would actually
bring him back.

The people around me cared and helped, 'Time' they said 'will mend,
the sadness that you feel right now, towards your special friend.'

My next companion was a ginger, who helped immensely with his purr,
The tinkle of his bell, even just the brush of his fur.

I know I couldn't have stopped it, it's just one of those things,
The few terrible tragedies, that life generally brings.

Even though I cannot see him, his body will never be here,
Nor are his cries and purr, but his spirit will always be near.

Julia Gibson (12)
South Hampstead High School

THE BULLY AND VICTIM

The bully stands proud.
The victim showers.

The bully, brain-dead.
The victim, a genius.

The bully appears bold and fearless.
The victim is numb with fright.

The bully, notorious for chewing gum.
The victim, known for his extensive vocabulary.

The bully, unethical.
The victim, scrupulous.

The bully, a powerful but callous mate.
The victim, a true though tedious friend.

The bully, once a victim.
The victim, soon to be a bully.

Georgina Cox (12)
South Hampstead High School

FRIENDS?

What is a friend?
I know a girl who calls herself my friend.
But she hurts me and lies to me,
So I call her a fiend.
What is the difference?

What is a friend?
I know another girl she calls herself a friend
And she is honest to me and kind
So I call her a true friend,
But what is the difference?

A fiend takes the side against you
She is not a friend.
But a true friend will always be
There for you when a friend goes against you.
She is someone special,
A *friend.*

Jessica Oughton (12)
South Hampstead High School

ESCAPE

'History lessons'
'What can you do?'
'Nothing very much'
'Just stare into space'
'Couldn't we skip it?'
'No she'll have a fit!'
'But it's so dull'
'We're doing the Normans'
'Battle of Hastings'
'William the conqueror'
'Boring'
'Dull'
'Dreary'
'Tedious'
'We could be ill?'
'Or have a fainting fit?'
'We could forget our books?'
'Or not hand in our homework?'
'No, it won't work!'
'History lessons'
'How to escape?'

Katherine Phoenix (12)
South Hampstead High School

London

Homeless wanderers, people, animals
roam the streets of busy London.
The noise is deafening, but they are used to it.
On their own, they are driven to steal.

Unknowing market sellers turn their backs on them.
The streams of endless people
are letting them go, unnoticed.

A child, attracted to an ice-cream stand,
slips away from his mother.
The crowd greedily snaps him up.
His mother cries out.
But he is gone.

A new homeless boy is on the streets,
No knowing his dreadful fate.
Suddenly he wants his mother.
He is scared.
But she is gone.
Forever.

People, covered in dirt and muck,
emerge out of their small houses.
The slums.
Unemployed, the parents walk the streets,
a look of slyness on their faces,
trying to find food.

They wander for hours on end,
rejected, they turn to stealing.
After dark, they return,
carrying an armful of supplies.

It is not enough.
You get what you are given.
Those are the rules.

The kids don't know how to behave.
They are now stuck in this life.

Forever.

Natasha Kahn (11)
South Hampstead High School

PROM NIGHT

I check if my dress is on straight.
Lipstick isn't smudged
I feel like a million dollars but
yet a little part of me is nervous
even frightened.

The sapphire on my dress glistens and sends
a ray of light which reflects onto the wall.
The night has finally arrived and
now that it is here I'm not sure
I can go through with it.
The magnificent crown sat on my dressing table
staring back at me.
Its beautiful silver lettering printed
Prom Queen made me feel special
I placed it on my head
and my heart swelled with pride.
At that moment in time I was proud to be me.

Hannah Gross (12)
South Hampstead High School

FRIENDSHIP

A mother is to be confided in,
Whilst sipping out of colourful mugs

A father is to be adored
And shared in warm bear hugs

A sister is to be gossiped with,
Till the very break of dawn

A brother is to be cherished,
From the moment that he is born

A cousin is to be valued
And plans with should be made

A pet is to be cuddled
And held close when you're afraid

A teacher is to be admired,
To help when you're unsure

A friend is to be treasured,
Forever and ever more.

Noor Nanji (12)
South Hampstead High School

MY VIEWS ON LONDON

People rush through crowded street not making contact with anything except the ground and their shopping bags.
Pollution fills the air as traffic mounts up in the street.
People shouting thinking they are more important than anyone else.
People rush in and out of shops carrying truckloads of bags.
Rushing in and out of shops like there is no tomorrow and everything has to be done today.
People sleeping rough on the streets beg for money as people walk past and look down on them with shame.

Parents with their children playing football in the park.
Groups of children playing on the swings or the slide.
Parents take their children for picnics in a park.
Children stop for a drink on their way to school.
As you walk past a church two people come out
looking happily married.
Children playing in the playground happily.

You can look at the world two ways a happy way or a miserable way. I prefer the happy way.

Siobhan Toone (11)
South Hampstead High School

FRIENDSHIP

Friendship is like a tree.
As it gets older
It grows, gets stronger,
Sways in the wind,
But doesn't fall.
The leaves flutter.
Some drop, others stay,
But the tree lives on.
Storms rip around it,
Pulling the branches,
Tearing at the roots.
But the tree stands,
Tall.
It will not die.
Whatever may come,
Real friendship lives on.
Forever.

Emma Hindley (12)
South Hampstead High School

DREAMS

Your defence is destroyed,
You are open, vulnerable.

Will you survive?
Should you give in?

The taunting envelopes you,
They are coming closer.

You are the black sheep,
In a field of white.

You feel the anger rising
And you shout, for equality,
Fairness and truth.

They realise - even understand.

But it's not that easy
Is it?

Louise Simpson (12)
South Hampstead High School

LONDON

L ights that glitter flooding the night sky
O xford Street's pavement crowded with shoppers.
N ightclubs throbbing with teenagers dancing
D rugs smuggled in bring sadness and death.
O n the pavement the homeless lie sleeping
N oisy car horns proclaiming pollution.

London is this and so much more -
home to me and many before.

Susannah Buckler (11)
South Hampstead High School

My Own London

The problem with traffic in London
Is that it stops you from going to school on time.
Swaying red double deckers,
Black taxis like scarab beetles
And many cars their colours like flowers in the grass.
The tube is a solution, quicker,
Like a snake rushing down a hole.

London has an invasion of pigeons
They seem to be like flying rats.
Diseased and dirty.
There are also lots of squirrels here,
They are mostly grey,
But in my country they are black or red.
Yesterday I saw a fox on my way to school.

My morning alarm clock is when horses come past,
They are returning from their morning exercise,
In Regent's Park.
The beat of their hooves are really relaxing sounds
When they are going back to their barracks.
They are arranged by their colour,
Pale brown going darker like milk chocolate bars.

No matter how long I live here
I will always be a tourist!

Milica Filimonovic (11)
South Hampstead High School

LONDON

Cats creep back towards their homes,
crawling through the dirty rubbish.
London is quiet,
no sounds can be heard.
The clock strikes four.

Birds sing their merry tunes whilst businessmen yawn
and stretch.
Sounds of traffic can be heard on the busy roads,
but the sun is still low on the horizon.
The clock strikes six.

Children chatter in the playgrounds,
sharing silly secrets.
People are shouting, brakes are squealing,
London so fully alive.
The clock strikes eight.

The sound of rain drumming on the rooftops,
of tall grey building that tower above the dirty streets.
Then the bright, warm sun casts a rainbow over
the beautifully well kept parks.
The clock strikes ten.

Inside restaurants, people discuss the morning's work,
happily munching on a burger or sandwich.
Outside stall holders call out,
Hoping for a hungry passer-by.
The clock strikes twelve.

Tourists clamber on to public transport,
ready to gasp at breathtaking sights.
Both children and adults are stewing over work,
waiting for the day to end.
The clock strikes two.

Children jump up as the bell rings,
marking the end of the day.
Outside the traffic is at its highest,
The horns sound like a modern brass orchestra!
The clock strikes four.

In families all over London
siblings argue over what they want for supper.
Mothers unsuccessfully persuade their children to eat their greens,
but they refuse this gruesome mush.
The clock strikes six.

Street lamps shine upon the grey city streets,
most shops have closed for the night.
Children are tucked up in bed and read their favourite bedtime story.
The clock strikes eight.

London is finally settling down,
lights switch off one by one.
The people fall asleep,
but the night creatures, awaken.
The clock strikes ten.

The night is silent but for a few drunk teenagers,
hobbling their way back home.
Darkness sweeps over like magic.
The clock strikes twelve.

People in their beds are dreaming about their busy days.
The clock strikes two.

Eva Tausig (11)
South Hampstead High School

LONDON FROM A CAR

Traffic snakes on for miles ahead
Pedestrians on the pavement seem worlds away
Then the grey sky opens
Melting the world into a mass of distorted shapes and colours.
Wipers struggle to keep up with the
constant drumming of rain pelting on the windscreen.

The door, lock and windscreen are the edge of the world,
like a metallic silver time capsule.

Traffic moves on, the car speeds up.

On the windscreen, the wipers are
catching up with the rain.
People are coming out of shops,
removing newspapers from their heads.
The rain is pattering more slowly and it
slows to a drizzle and fades away.

Ruthie Samuel (11)
South Hampstead High School

LONDON IN THE WINTER

Busy people scurry.
Rain beating down.
Icy hands shiver;
Never escaping from the cold

Smoky London,
Bulging traffic.
Polluted air,
Noisy car horns.

Huge buildings,
Ever towering over me.
Above this dray city,
Of cold and damp

Busy people scurry,
Rain beating down.
Icy hands shiver,
Never escaping from the cold.

Rebecca Moodey (11)
South Hampstead High School

THIS IS LONDON

Hustle and bustle, the crowding of streets,
The honking of horns, the shuffling of feet.
The cars are creating a lot of pollution,
And there is lots of smog down in the station.
The sun is sinking a patchwork on the ground,
Because we march through the streets as a very big crowd
stop!
Refrain
Down in the alley we hear tin clattering,
Up in the sky the clouds are scattering,
Along the street litter is rushing,
It's very cold and rain is gushing,
After all this is London
After all this *is* London

Doors swinging in and out,
People in and out.
Signs say left and right
People *going* left and right
stop!

Laura Elvin (12)
South Hampstead High School

WINTER'S GIFT

A cold winter evening,
The streets are dead
And the rain is beating, beating, beating.
The shops are deserted,
No cars on the road
And the rain is beating, beating, beating.
A rumble of thunder,
A flash of lightning
And the rain is beating, beating, beating.
Hands like icecubes,
Feet like snow
And the rain is beating no end to show.
Then a swish and a swerve
And the peace is disturbed.
A blur of red and orange,
Glowing through the gloom,
An array of piercing colours
The inviting warmth,
The bus is towering down on me
Like a fire against a sooty chimney
And the stars against the night sky
This shelter protects me from the storm
A utopia so colourful and bright.

Rachel Stratton (12)
South Hampstead High School

LONDON

A sea of traffic crowds the streets, with people here and there.
The sky opens up and shows the light, the morning is complete.

The day continues, the traffic calms and the cloud with the silver lining disappears to show the sun.

Businesses open as usual, it's just ordinary day. Except for that smile that's smiling at me, a long, long way away.

Lunchtime means business, well . . . for some in a way.
Though for others it's just the relaxing part of the day.
The screeching of the cars returns,
as do the people, littering the streets.

Midday passes and schools start their break. The blue sky remains as the crowds fade away.

Silence is near to filling the air but as time rattles on that memory is gone as London city is once again filled with life.
The evening approaches.

As the evening turns into the night, the hum of traffic
and the rattle of the train quieten.
Though London is never *black*.
There is always the odd light showing us the way.

Sarah Bolsom-Morris (11)
South Hampstead High School

THE TRAIN

The train caterwauls through the tunnel,
The engine wires fuse and explode in delighted cataclysms
                                        of dancing sparks,
Settling down,
The engine purrs contentedly.

The train moves through the endless chasms of the
                                London Underground,
The sombre, inky-black walls illuminated only by occasional
                                        bright white posters.

Outside,
The world swirls in a flurry of commotion and sounds.

Underground,
People count their change and look distractedly at their watches,
Guitar notes echo softly through the scattered corridors
And a drunken man moves, swaying, through the thickening throngs
                                        of waiting people,
Staring silently down the never-terminating tunnel,
Waiting.

A swift rush of air,
A shower of dust,
A faint scent of diesel
And an eruption of light, dirt and noise,
Signifies the entrance of the train.

It swallows the crowd,
Filling its hungry belly as it crams the rush-hour rabble into
                                        its empty carriages.

The train,
Rushing.
Gushing desultory passengers through its doors onto
                                          the dingy platforms,
Hurtling through the blackness,
Towards Chiswick.

Jessie Lieberson (12)
South Hampstead High School

LONDON

Sitting in the dirty red bus
wondering if I would ever reach home.
The blazing sun shone through the dirty windows
as I sat there all alone.
I looked outside, all I could see
was a blanket of cars covering up the street.
So I sat down and lay back in my seat.
I could hear horns of cars and the engine
of the double decker bus going rumble, rumble.
As we moved only an inch we stopped with a stumble.
The traffic lights ahead brightened up the gloomy streets,
it almost worked like a sweetener.
We drove past the filthy waters of the Thames,
which was polluted with litter by careless Londoners.
We passed Big Ben as the clock struck five *dong*.
I had finally reached my destination.
I walked down the steep stairs.
The doors flapped open as I walked onto the dirty streets of London.

Sara Nielsen-Dzumhur (11)
South Hampstead High School

LONDON

The airport

A scramble of people waiting for taxis,
Each claiming that they arrived at the rank first.
Many corridors and passageways just to get to the right gate,
To find out later you are an hour delayed.
Adults shoving to claim all their luggage,
This is the hum of the London Airport.

The tube station

Tired people returning from work,
With large briefcases and bags hanging below their tired eyes.
Then all at once as the tube draws near
And the blue doors open,
People push out and people push in,
No courtesy have the citizens of London.

The bus stop

Endless waits at the various bus stops,
You pay your fare and you climb aboard,
Then you sit down next to a granny, man or woman.
People of all different shapes and sizes,
You view them all here on the bus.
These are the citizens from the city of London.

The rush hour

Angry mothers in their cars hooting,
Racing to pick the kids up from school,
Chatting endlessly on their mobiles,
Flicking their hair,
While shouting at fellow drivers,
Claiming that they are a good hour late.

The mothers

Having coffee mornings here and there,
Racing to the phone,
Off to the shops,
They have no time for business
Only rushing here and there in their great people movers,
These are the mothers of the city of London.

The fathers

Waking up early and tuning in to the early morning news,
While eating their health food,
They're cooking your omelette,
Then dash off to work in a horrible mood,
Arriving home in the dark in even more of a gloom,
These are the fathers of the city of London.

Jessica Howard (11)
South Hampstead High School

LONDON

I worm my way through London crowds, to see the famous
Oxford Street before me,
The look of the shops compel me, no matter what they sell,
Cinemas showing nearly every film,
Different people surrounding me,
All these things make me proud to live in London.
I realise there's another side to London,
The miserable side that I can't escape from.
I try not to breathe in all the fumes,
The noisy traffic gives me a headache,
The strange people circling me, giving me looks,
And then I see the homeless on the streets,
The perfect London, now I think, does not exist.

Elizabeth Metliss (11)
South Hampstead High School

CITIES AND POLLUTION

In cities the main problem is often car traffic,
As there are far too many cars on the roads.
The cars are also giving off fumes
And the pollution is destroying the ozone layer.

In cities there are many shops,
For people to buy food, clothes, books.
Many more shops are opening
And some are going out of business.
The same is happening to restaurants, pubs, and cafes.

There are parks to cycle in
And where children climb up trees,
But the bins are not being used
And litter is being thrown on the ground.

The modern world is based on technology
And in order to build high-powered machines
Like computers, mobile phones and televisions,
We need more factories and office buildings,
Which then pollute the world's atmosphere.

Entertainment in major cities like Manchester is really *big,*
There are lots of cinemas, bowling alleys,
Ice-skating rinks, swimming and leisure centres,
Theatres, football clubs and much more.

When we see tourism we see London,
For instance some buildings that attract tourists are
Big Ben, Tower Bridge, Buckingham Palace.
Places like London Aquarium, Trafalgar Square,
Madam Tussaud's and London zoo.

Georgina Ely (11)
South Hampstead High School

LONDON, A FOOL'S PARADISE!

I sniffed the pollution in the morning air,
I was flabbergasted to see my beloved city in such a state.
Buses were galumphing and intimidating,
The rush hour was horrendous.
London was alive again!

The monuments and streets were open to the public and
tourists who flock in their millions,
Oxford Street, Piccadilly Circus, Leicester Square and London Bridge,
greatest of them all.
Entertainers achieved plenty of money playing music and
juggling on the roads,
All the shopping centres and the unique and delightful covered market.
London was alive again!

When I visit the city centre my senses are filled with a heady
cocktail of bleating horns and diesel particulate,
Where man and machine literally rubbed shoulders.
After a while, it is a great relief to return to the peace and
tranquillity of the suburbs.
London has always been a popular destination of immigrants
from across the world.

Romans, Vikings, Normans and Anglo-Saxons have all come and
settled in.
Recently, Africans and Asian settlers have made this city
a truly multi-cultural capital of the world.
London has been the financial capital of the world in the #
last millennium
And always will be!

Ishita Menta (12)
South Hampstead High School

Listen To London Sleep

Come rest now and close your weary eyes,
Listen to the silence, the sombre silence, the rare silence,
Listen to the darkness,
Listen, listen
Listen to London sleep.

Listen to the beggars seal their pale, withered eyes,
Listen to the workmen finally shut their tool boxes,
Listen to the hum of the traffic die down,
Listen, listen,
Listen to London sleep.

Listen to Big Ben strike each hour,
Listen to the street lamps flicker pale light,
Listen to shops close up for the night,
Listen, listen,
Listen to London sleep.

Listen to the humour from the theatre,
Listen to pollution scatter through the air,
Listen to the wet graffiti trickle down the wall,
Listen, listen,
Listen to London sleep.

Listen to animals creep around the gutters,
Listen to restaurants serve their last customers,
Listen to drunks stagger along the street,
Listen, listen,
Listen to London sleep.

Listen to the silence, the sombre silence, the rare silence,
Listen to the darkness,
Listen, listen,
Listen to London sleep . . .

Emily Zitcer (11)
South Hampstead High School

People In London

People rushing, always rushing,
This way, that way,
Forwards, backwards,
Through the drizzling rain.

Babies, children, mothers, fathers,
This way, that way,
Forwards, backwards,
Through the howling wind.

Crowds yelling, children screaming,
This way, that way,
Forwards, backwards,
Through the crashing thunder.

This is people.

Rachel Lob-Levyt (11)
South Hampstead High School

Dream

One eats
One sleeps
One has warmth
And is awarded for anything he does

One is hungry
One can't sleep
One struggles for his life

I dream one day that there will be an end to this
or is my dream a dream of a faint fantasy of a
pleasant world of an unending path.

Harun Abdi Hassan
White Hart Lane School

As I Walk Through The Dark...

As I walk through the dark and lonely night
something shiny catches my eye, oh it's just a Cola can.
As I wander down an alley the wind is howling with its might,
a cat jumps out of a dumpster and gives me a fright.
As I trudge through the autumn leaves a car passes by,
at such a late hour I wonder why?
As I step along gravel it gives a crunching sound,
it echoes all around me round and round.
As I walk down the road some lights click on in a house
a dog starts howling and people start to shout.
As I struggle through the woods my foot gets caught on a tree root,
I trip and fall with a tumble.
As I start towards my house I see Christmas lights,
the decorations in Oxford Street seem so pretty and bright.
As I arrive at my door the moon beams down upon me
as a cloud comes to cover it up.
Finally I sit in my favourite chair then I have some hot chocolate
in my favourite cup.
I climb up the stairs tired and half awake. I fall about and shake.
As I reach my bed and climb in and it's so cosy and warm
and when I'm snoring I sound like a thunder storm.

Kazan Tawfiq (11)
White Hart Lane School

Sunrise

As the light grew bright
I awoke to the morning light
As I got up out of bed
The Lord is the first, I thank in my head.

The birds start to sing
The fish start to swim
Everything has woken
That's what the sunrise brings.

Jamila Cunningham (11)
White Hart Lane School

WRESTLING

I watch those big,
Giants fight.
Angry faces,
Showing off their might.

Famous names like
Sting and stone cold.
To go in that ring,
You've got to be pretty bold.

They're tough, they're
Hard they're super fast.
Their punches,
Are like lightning blasts.

High flyers jump high,
From ropes.
They get hurt
I don't know how they cope.

Heavyweights,
Are as strong as bears.
Get one angry,
Just say your prayers.

Rasika Amarasinghe (13)
White Hart Lane School

WHAT SHALL I DO?

'It started in the morning,
My mum woke me up for school,
I got up very sleepy mumbling to myself,
I look at the mirror in a fright,
I saw a spot in the centre of my nose,
It was big and brightly red
It was as red as if I had painted my nose.
I looked like a dummy,
I didn't know what to do!
I was scared to go to school,
I might get bullied,
Or even I might be cussed,

Shall I pretend I fell sick?
Or shall I pretend I forgot school?

What shall I do?'

Jennifer Kan (11)
White Hart Lane School

THE TEACHER WEATHER FORECAST

Mrs Lambret will reach gale force when she hits the playground.

Mr Smith will be rather windy especially after lunchtime.

Mrs Dragon will be rather hot and sunny when she finds
out the gas has been left on.

Mr Kallon will be quite rainy after the number jumble in his head.

Mrs Ram will be thundering around like mad when she finds out
the Canary Wharf has been knocked down.

Sibel Sonara (11)
White Hart Lane School

I Have A Dream

I have a dream that I could be slim,
So I could wear clothes that made me look glim.
I wear long coats and baggy trousers
So no one knows I've got big fat thighses.
I had a dream that I was Naomi Campbell,
I get cursed and troubled by boys at school
But I cursed them back 'cause I'm no fool.
Oh I wish, I wish that I could be slim
So I can look like little Kim.
With slim thighs and a beautiful face
But that's impossible 'cause I eat sugary sweet lace.
As I walk day by day
With my mum to Holloway.
As I reach home sweet home
My belly feels like the London Dome,
All big and empty and it bubbles inside.
I tried to find the crisps which my mum always hides
But she hides them very well indeed
So I have tuna, oh that's my greed.
When I'm at school the boys come up to me they call me 'Hippo'
And all kinds of things to create their fun
But when I get angry they start to run
But I do, I do wish to be slim
So I can wear clothes that look so glim.
I have a dream
But one day I will be slim
And I'll show those boys that I too can be slim.

Laamaray Rhoden (13)
White Hart Lane School

CHASE

(A tribute poem to my five year old cousin Chase who died of meningitis, 10th February 1999)

Chase was so special, special to all he was so cute, honest, innocent and small.
The smile on his face that he always wore.
He was mainly happy and sweet, hardly bitter and sore.
His face was so beautiful, gentle and mild,
eyes so wide with the innocence of a child.
His heart was so able, able to love. He was such an angel, a gift from above, a parcel from heaven and now he's returned.,
only by soul and maybe by heart but if we don't forget Chase, we'll never be apart.
We love you forever Chase, even in death we'll always remember you, never forget.

Siohvan Cleo Crombie (13)
White Hart Lane School

TEACHER'S PRAYER

Let the children in our care
Clean their shoes and comb their hair
Come to school on time and be neat
Blow their noses and wipe their feet.
Let them Lord not eat in class
Or rush in the hall en masse.
Let them show some self control
Let them slow down, let them stroll!

Let the children in our charge
Not be violent or large.
Not be sick on the school trip bus
Not be cleverer than us.
Not be unwashed, loud or mad
(With a six foot mother or a seven foot dad).
Let them please say 'drew' not 'drawed'
Let them know the answer Lord!

Shubhana Zubair Mohammed (11)
White Hart Lane School

PEACE

What more can a person wish for
In this lifetime you have to all expect peace.
You hear from the fast bombing
From the west earthquakes.
North shooting.
South children are dying from starvation.
If only it could all just stop.
As a child all you want is to be able to go outside and play
But you can't.
Parents worried as soon as you leave the house that you are not
Coming back.
Being a girl makes it worse.
Your mother thinking her little girl is getting raped.
It is terrible.
The world is turning to a trash tin. Filled with rubbish.
The rotten getting over the pure.
We have to do something before it gets any worse.
Without peace we can't survive in this world.
Peace we have to get it back.

Mary Sofolabo (14)
White Hart Lane School